The Cosmic Factor

The Cosmic Factor

Health and Astrology

James Vogh

GRANADA
London Toronto Sydney New York

Published by Granada Publishing in
Hart-Davis, MacGibbon Ltd 1978
Reprinted by Granada Publishing 1979

Granada Publishing Limited
Frogmore, St Albans, Herts AL2 2NF
and
3 Upper James Street, London W1R 4BP
866 United Nations Plaza, New York, NY 10017, USA
Q164 Queen Victoria Buildings, Sydney, NSW 2000, Australia
100 Skyway Avenue, Rexdale, Ontario M9W 3A6, Canada
PO Box 84165, Greenside, 2034 Johannesburg, South Africa
CML Centre, Queen & Wyndham, Auckland 1, New Zealand

ISBN 0 246 10989 0

Printed in Great Britain by
Richard Clay (The Chaucer Press) Ltd,
Bungay, Suffolk

GRANADA PUBLISHING ®

Contents

PART ONE
Principles

Introduction

No one can say for certain why Elvis Presley suffered a fatal heart attack on 16 August 1977, or why Bing Crosby was struck down by an identical heart attack two months later. But the health astrologer, looking at the birth charts of both men, is bound to notice certain strange similarities.

Both were born with Saturn in Aquarius. For both, Saturn was also 'ill-aspected' by other planets (the term may sound vague, but it has a precise mathematical meaning). Traditionally, this can mean heart trouble, especially during times when Saturn happens to occupy the sign *opposite* Aquarius. That sign is Leo, traditional ruler of the heart.

When Elvis Presley suffered his heart attack, Saturn was in Leo. And Saturn was in Leo on 14 October when Bing Crosby died.

Naturally all this could be a tremendous coincidence.* So could the New Moon exactly two days before Elvis's attack, and the New Moon (*and* eclipse) exactly two days before Bing's attack. On the other hand, this could all be one glimpse of a cosmic pattern that affects all of us, in our lives and in our health. If such a pattern exists – and the evidence is stronger than you might suspect – then the key to its understanding may be astrology.

A few years ago no respectable scientist dared take astrology seriously. It seemed incredible that planets millions of miles away could have any real effect on human health or character. Science preferred simple mechanistic explanations: the solar system as a clockwork arrangement of sterile planets; human behaviour as a set of mechanical reflexes, life itself as a molecular accident. Astrologers, by

* The odds against this coincidence are over 580,000 to 1.

9

contrast, kept insisting on pattern and meaning in the universe. The simple mechanisms of science were not enough. There had to be more – a 'cosmic factor' uniting the larger pattern of stars and planets with the smaller pattern of life. They could not explain this cosmic factor in terms of hard science, but they knew it existed: a kind of radiation reaching from other planets to affect life on earth.

Scientists ridiculed the idea of a cosmic factor – until they themselves began to find evidence for it. Space probes showed the planets to be 'alive', pulsating with electromagnetic energy. Their radiation reaches even to the Earth, and their movements weave a complex energy pattern over its surface, unique at every point in time, unique at every place.

What is more important, the cosmic factor does affect us. In 1938 a Japanese doctor, Maki Takata, discovered that the composition of human blood changes radically during an eclipse. In the 1950s a Belgian statistician showed that persons successful in a given profession are likely to have been born when a certain planet was prominent in the sky – and unlikely to have been born at other times. In 1968 a group of Czech doctors completed a year-long test of 'astrological birth control': Out of 1252 women patients who tried it, only twenty-eight became pregnant. In 1977 a London professor of psychology demonstrated that zodiac signs have measurable effects on human personality.

These are only a few highlights, but they show a change in the scientific outlook. Each in his own compartment of specialization, scientists are now forging the links of evidence into a solid chain leading to only one conclusion: Human life and health are deeply affected by the cosmic factor.

Astrologers have never doubted this. It is a vision to which they have remained true for the past forty centuries. But the fact that science is now beginning to recognize it as a valid vision is nevertheless encouraging. It promises new research, leading ultimately to the birth of a new science, *bioastrology*: The study of the cosmic factor in human health (physical, mental and psychical).

This book is intended to explore in advance the fascinating field of bioastrology. It will seek answers to far-ranging questions about health and the stars:

How do Sun signs affect your health? Who is prone to smoking, who to over-eating, and who to stress diseases? How do biorhythms figure in the horoscope? Are sunspots linked to heart disease? Can the Moon somehow cause 'madness'? Can illness be foreseen and avoided? Exactly how does astrological birth control work?

Often such questions have no clear, short answers. The bioastrologer must read the birth chart with care, taking account of the complete pattern as well as isolated indications. Snap decisions must be avoided, for the pattern of the stars is not always what it seems at first glance.

Obviously not everyone born with a planetary predisposition to heart disease will actually have a heart attack. Nor will every heavy smoker contract lung cancer. Much depends upon general health, diet, stress, exercise and many other factors. A sensible life style and proper awareness of potential health problems can often help prevent their becoming actual health problems.

Here too bioastrology may help, by providing guidelines for preventive health care, through health awareness. Surely if someone knows he has a predisposition to, say, stress diseases, he is better equipped to avoid stressful situations and preserve his health.

This book is aimed primarily at the layman who takes health matters seriously – though the professional astrologer may also find in it useful information not easily available elsewhere. Part One, *Principles*, explains the meaning of the zodiac and planets in the health horoscope. Each chapter covers a single basic principle, relating ancient traditions to modern methods.

Part Two, *Signs of Life*, takes up the practical use of Sun signs, Moon signs and Rising signs. Each chapter is devoted to a single sign, with the physical, mental and emotional traits explained at some depth. Each covers immunity or susceptibility to certain diseases, appropriate herbal remedies and cell-salts, and the detection of biorhythm danger-days for the Sun sign in question. A final chapter is devoted to the 'psychic' sign, Arachne.

Part Three, *Planets and Aspects*, explains step by step how to read the medical birth chart, interpreting the influence of planets, houses and aspects, checking the overall pattern, and integrating all of this into a comprehensive health reading.

Part Four, *Alternatives and Refinements*, is designed for the bioastrologer who wishes to go further into other traditions. It covers Chinese astrology in relation to herbalism and acupuncture; the Vedic system in India; the Aztec 'calendar of health'; body charting and biorhythms. These are not meant to be rivals to the Western tradition, but helpful complements. They may be of particular use in resolving difficult or ambiguous horoscopes, or in adding to the predictive power of a reading.

Does bioastrology work? The reader can find out for himself only by trying it, as the ancients of Mesopotamia, and a few modern scientists, have tried it. He may, like them, discover the cosmic factor.

CHAPTER ONE

Zodiac Man

Most of us know there is a zodiac of twelve signs, and that each is supposed to affect those 'born under' it in a unique way. Those born under a certain sign are said to share a certain character or 'type'. If for example you are born between 21 March and 19 April your sign is Aries, the Ram, which ought to make you headstrong, bold, adventurous, better at leading than following.

Astrology has never been this simple, but let's imagine for the moment that it is, and introduce the twelve signs.

Aries, the Ram (21 March to 19 April) signifies a person who is 'in feats of Warre and Courage invincible, scorning any should exceed him, subject to no Reason, Bold . . .'* (Examples: General Westmoreland, Bismarck, Lenin, Khrushchev.)

Taurus, the Bull (20 April to 20 May) 'signifies a quiet man . . . Loving Mirth in his words and actions . . . Zealous in their affections, Musicall . . .' (Perry Como, Brahms, Tchaikovsky, Bing Crosby, Fred Astaire.)

Gemini, the Twins (21 May to 21 June) 'represents a man of a subtill and politick braine . . . using much eloquence in his speech . . . sharp and witty'. (Henry Kissinger, John F. Kennedy, Thomas Hardy.)

Cancer, the Crab (22 June to 21 July) is the hermit or banker type: secretive, frugal, prudent, solitary, and 'loving Peace, and to live free from the cares of this Life'. (Thoreau, Nathaniel Hawthorne, John D. Rockefeller, Jacques Cousteau.)

Leo, the Lion (22 July to 21 August) is the executive type:

* The quotations, for all signs, are taken from a text by the astrologer William Lilly, published in 1647.

open, expansive, bossy, having 'a kind of itching desire to Rule . . . of great Majesty and Statelinesse . . .' (Napoleon, Robert Redford, George Bernard Shaw, Fidel Castro.)

Virgo, the Virgin (22 August to 22 September) is the helper: modest, careful, accurate, discreet, giving great attention to detail. (Peter Sellers, Greta Garbo, Ingres, the instrument-maker Helmholtz, the scientist Rutherford.)

Libra, the Scales (23 September to 22 October) is the diplomat type: balanced, reasonable, mathematical, fair-minded, and often musical. (Pierre Trudeau, Eisenhower, Gandhi, Franz Liszt.)

Scorpio, the Scorpion (23 October to 21 November) is the soldier type: aggressive, brave, stubborn, 'lovers of Warre and things pertaining thereunto, hazarding himself to all Perils . . .' (Generals Patton and Montgomery, Picasso, Billy Graham, Marie Curie.)

Sagittarius, the Archer (22 November to 21 December) is the priest type: far-sighted, visionary, enthusiastic, aspiring and 'preachy'. (Walt Disney, de Gaulle, Beethoven, Andrew Carnegie, Mark Twain.)

Capricorn, the Sea-Goat (22 December to 20 January) is the organizer: economical, persevering, self-critical and ambitious. 'He is profound in imagination, in his acts severe, in his words reserved, in speaking and giving very spare, in labour patient . . .' (Richard Nixon, Mao Tse-tung, Elvis Presley, Albert Schweitzer, Muhammad Ali, Howard Hughes.)

Aquarius, the Water-man (20 January to 19 February) is the scientist or reformer: progressive, inventive, humanitarian. (Lincoln, Darwin, Byron, F. D. Roosevelt, Lewis Carroll.)

Pisces, the Two Fish (20 February to 21 March) is the nurse type: self-sacrificing, mystical, believing, caring. (Ralph Nader, Chopin, Vanessa Redgrave, Pius XII, Rimsky-Korsakov, Alexander Graham Bell.)

The problem with such lists is that there are obviously more than twelve kinds of people in the world. Some people fit their signs very well (Napoleon certainly had the Leonine

14

itch to rule). Others do not seem to fit their signs at all (Muhammad Ali could never be called 'spare' of speech). Does this mean that the zodiac is arbitrary and meaningless? Does it mean that astrology is 'bunk'?

Far from it. Sorting people according to their signs (in this case, their Sun signs) may be fun, but it's hardly genuine astrology. No one would think highly of a pharmacist, say, who could only sort pills into heaps of pink, white and green. Neither should anyone take too seriously the advice of a newspaper 'horoscope' which sorts people into just twelve heaps. Genuine astrology is more complex, but also more rewarding.

To set up the natal horoscope, or birth chart, of an individual, the astrologer must know his exact year, month and day of birth (if possible the exact hour and minute) and the place of birth. These allow the astrologer to determine the unique pattern of the planets for that individual (called the 'Native' of the horoscope). The pattern changes from moment to moment and from place to place, so that every birth chart is as individual as a fingerprint. Even twins, if born minutes apart, have slightly different charts. Your 'stars' are truly yours, for no one else can be born with your exact birth chart for at least 25,000 years.

Nevertheless, persons born near the same time often seem to lead remarkably similar lives:

Albert Einstein and Otto Hahn were born 14 March 1879. Both became physicists, both worked on atomic theory, and both were awarded the Nobel prize.

Two of the most sensual artists of the past century, Claude Monet and Auguste Rodin, were born on 14 November 1840. In 1900, when Monet exhibited his most famous painting, *Water Lilies*, Rodin also held the exhibition that established his reputation. In 1902 both men again produced major works.

Lauritz Melchior and Benjamin Gigli were born on 20 March 1890. Both became popular tenors, and both joined the New York Metropolitan Opera.

Edward Fitzgerald and Nicolai Gogol were both born 31 March 1809. Fitzgerald made his reputation by translating

The Rubaiyat of Omar Khayyam from the Persian. Gogol first made his reputation by translating folk tales from the Ukrainian. Both suffered illnesses at the same time. In February 1844 Fitzgerald wrote: 'Travelling, you know, is a vanity. The *soul* remains the same.' Two months later, Gogol wrote: 'I am perfectly indifferent to my surroundings. Most of the time I travel only to meet the people whose presence my soul requires.'

The Irish writers James Joyce and James Stephens were both born on the morning of 2 February 1889. Their photographs[1] show them to be virtually physical twins, and their works show an identical, compulsively careful use of language.

Many more such cases of 'time twins' are listed elsewhere,[2] more than enough to establish the correlation between a person's time and place of birth and his physical, mental and psychical life.

If such time patterns exist, there must be a basis for their existence. The basis for all time patterns in astrology is the zodiac.

The word 'zodiac' comes from the Greek *zodiakos* ('circle of animals') and the zodiac has always been shown as a circle of real or mythical animals, the world over. The circle represents a cycle in time, but also in space: There is a real circle of constellations girdling the sky, marking the path of the Sun, Moon and planets. This path is divided into twelve equal segments, each named for one of these constellations. In late March, the Sun is actually in that part of the sky we call Aries. As the Earth moves along its orbit, the Sun appears to move against the background of stars, until (a month later) it is in Taurus. It takes exactly a year for the Sun to transit all of the signs and complete the cycle; indeed, this is how the year is defined. Likewise the month is defined by the time it takes the fast-moving Moon to complete the cycle of the zodiac (about twenty-eight days). These and other cycles have real, measurable effects on earthly life of all kinds.

Since the Sun grows our plants, and since plant growth is one of the more obvious life processes on Earth, there is at least one connection between celestial bodies and life. Another is the annual cycle of seasons – that is, the Sun's cycle of the zodiac, as seen from Earth. Crocuses usually bloom when the Sun is in Pisces. When the Sun enters Capricorn, hedgehogs enter their burrows to hibernate.

Most biological clocks are timed by the Sun or Moon or both. Dormice kept in a windowless laboratory for months still awaken at sunset every night, prowl their cages until just before dawn, and then go back to sleep. Even germinating beans become 'restless' when the Moon is up.[3]

Long before the solar–lunar computer at Stonehenge was conceived, Nature implanted similar computers in quite primitive animal brains. The simple marine worm *Eunice viridis* breeds only once a year, and every member of this species in the South Pacific breeds at exactly the same moment: 'at dawn on the day the moon reaches its last quarter in November'.[4]

The indigo bunting, a North American songbird, uses an even more remarkable computer. It migrates 2000 miles from New England to a Caribbean island with perfect precision, flying mostly at night. A night flight over the ocean rules out both landmarks and the Sun as guidance, so that ornithologists were unable to explain how the bunting found its way. Then in 1967 Dr Stephen Emlen tested buntings under the artificial night sky of a planetarium. He discovered that these birds steer by the star Polaris.[5]

Man too is a part of Nature, and ruled or guided by celestial events. The difference is, man can use his intelligence to attempt to understand these events: 32,000 years ago, Ice Age people began scratching upon pieces of bone a record of the phases of the Moon.

Almost certainly early men studied the seasons, if only to be able to predict changes in their food supply. They also learned to mark the seasons by the Sun's position relative to certain stars. For example, the Egyptians knew that when Sirius rises with the Sun, the spring flooding of the Nile is at hand.

Eventually men learned that the Sun passes continually along the same belt of sky, blotting out the same constellations in the same order each year. In spring, the Sun seemed to pass through the constellation we call Aries, the Ram; then Taurus, the Bull and so on. In different places the stars were grouped differently and called by different names, but the principle was always the same: At each time of year, the Sun has its accustomed place.

They also noticed that people born at different times of year were characteristically different. A child born in late winter was likely to be weak, undersized and susceptible to disease, while one born only a few weeks later, in spring, might be strong, hardy and disease-resistant.

This is crude, and very far from the present-day principles of astrology, yet even this can be tested. Dr Lyall Watson feels there may be a 'fundamental biological principle involved, because children born during May are, on the average, about two hundred grams heavier than those born in any other month'.[6]

Bioastrology could not make great advances until (about 10,000 BC) nomadic hunting tribes began settling into farming communities, which in turn began to draw together into the first civilizations. For the first time, men had the leisure to study the stars carefully and for the first time they had the writing and mathematics to make sense of what they saw, and the ability to record long-range predictions. Moreover, the need for bioastrology was great. They studied the conditions that would help predict great disasters that had never troubled simple nomads: crop failure, epidemics, cattle plague. As the king became responsible for more and more people, it became more and more important to know all about his physical and mental health. In time, bioastrologers would search for the answers to deeper questions, seeking the meaning of life itself in the pattern of the cosmos.

All of this contributed to the advance of this early science, but one aspect of neolithic farming life made bioastrology possible. Living in fixed communities, men could now build fixed observatories, without which they could never have come to understand the stars.

By now, almost everyone has heard that Stonehenge was an

astronomical computer. It was built, we're told, about 3000 BC. Massive stones were quarried hundreds of miles away and hauled to the site, and set up to align with certain critical positions of the Sun and Moon. It is surrounded by a ring of fifty-six holes which, when used with markers, can be employed to predict future eclipses.

What is surprising, however, is that Stonehenge was also a kind of clinic or healing centre. Geoffrey of Monmouth, writing in the twelfth century, repeats a curious legend about the builders of Stonehenge: '. . . whenever they felt ill, baths should be prepared at the foot of the stones; for they used to pour water over them and run this water into baths in which their sick were cured. What is more, they mixed the water with herbal concoctions, and so healed their wounds. There isn't a single stone among them that hasn't some medicinal virtue.'[7]

Apparently those who built the monument saw some connection between studying the stars and healing the sick. The same connection occurred to others, including the father of rational medicine, Hippocrates: 'Astronomy contributes not the least but truly the most to medicine. For if anyone comprehends the changes of the times and the rise and decline of the stars, he will foresee and prognosticate . . .'[8]

Stonehenge was used to foresee eclipses. In ancient times, eclipses were believed to cause all sorts of evils, from blindness and skin diseases to flood tides, river pollution and great wars.[9] This may at first sound like superstition, but when we come to look at these afflictions one at a time, they seem at least possible: People do go blind from staring at solar eclipses. Bathing in polluted rivers can easily cause skin and eye infections. Eclipses do cause flood tides (through the combined gravitation of Sun and Moon) which in turn stir up river deltas, causing pollution.

That leaves only war. There is a surprising amount of evidence in favour of a connection between wars and eclipses. Eclipses occur at intervals of fifty-seven years (eg, there was an eclipse on 8 June 1899, and another on 8 June 1956) and this cycle is shown in the Stonehenge eclipse-computer.

And according to the Foundation for the Study of Cycles, there is also a fifty-seven-year cycle of 'international battles',[10] over several centuries. Elsewhere astrologer Joseph Goodavage points out that: 'Military commanders of both ancient and modern times have noticed the tendency for mass troop movements to follow each eclipse. Some of these troop movements actually followed the line of the eclipse's path.'[11] This is true: Alfred the Great stopped the invading Vikings along such a line on 2 November 878, while in 1945 the American First Army halted along another such line to allow Russian troops to enter East Germany.

It would seem that the Celts who built Stonehenge had at least two excellent reasons to be concerned about eclipses: public health and public safety. Their astronomer-physicians would be likely to prescribe sensible treatments for eye infections, skin infections and war wounds, including the baths mentioned by Geoffrey of Monmouth. Healing baths were a popular treatment in the Celtic world, especially in this locality. The area about Stonehenge abounds in ancient holy wells and springs, known from antiquity to have medicinal properties.

Twenty-five miles away is the city of Bath, whose origins are traced to Celtic legend. It is said that a Prince Bladud, who practised the 'magical' arts of medicine and astrology, placed 'a cunning stone as big as a tree . . . in the welling spring, and that made the water hot and healed the sick people'.[12] Modern analysis shows these waters to contain beneficial salts of magnesium and sodium, as well as traces of radon and radium.[13] The waters are mildly radioactive, having passed over a rare type of stone – so perhaps there is something in the Bladud legend after all.*

Stonehenge and Bath are only two out of many hundreds of Celtic sacred sites – such as Wells, Winchester, Avebury, Glastonbury – associated with healing and with the stars. These sites may provide an explanation of *how* the stars affect life on Earth.

* The Greeks knew Bladud under his Druidic name, Abaris, and believed him to be a magician who could banish epidemics (see p. 60).

To begin with, these sites are aligned with one another, with three, five or even ten sites standing on a single line that cuts across miles of countryside. Taken together, these hundreds of sites form a vast network of straight lines. Though this network has been discovered many times (in 1648, 1920 and 1938, at least)[14] it has only recently been explained.

Various writers[15] suggest that these lines follow currents of the earth's magnetic force. Geomagnetism apparently has biological effects: 'A "healing centre" is really a centre of intense beneficial electromagnetic activity: Birds and animals are attracted to it in large numbers, people find it a soothing and pleasant *ambiance*, and often its very stones or waters become imbued with health-giving properties. Lourdes, Malvern, Bath, Marienbad come to mind . . .'[16]

If there are such centres of 'positive' force, we might also expect there to be centres of 'negative' force, known to be exceptionally dangerous, destructive of life or unpleasant. There do seem to be several such spots on our magnetic planet, notably the notorious Bermuda Triangle: Five researchers are now looking into 'magnetic peculiarities' typified by this mysterious area.[17] *New Scientist* recently reported a similar danger-zone in Wales, the 'Llandudno Pentagon', where people have been vanishing regularly since the twelfth century.[18] Still another is the 'Oregon Vortex', a circular area (just the size of Stonehenge) near Grant's Pass, Oregon. Within it, objects actually roll uphill, pendulums refuse to hang straight down and trees grow towards magnetic North. Birds and animals avoid the area, while humans who enter it feel 'a tremendous pull downward, as though gravity had been intensified. You instinctively lean at an angle of about ten degrees towards the centre of the circle.'[19] In other words, we can sense the 'wrongness' of such a centre of negative forces. Sensing the 'rightness' of a *positive* centre is not always so easy; people often seem to require aids, such as the dowsing rod. The late Guy Underwood, a retired lawyer interested in dowsing, tested Stonehenge and found it to be the centre of a tight spiral of underground forces. He found similar patterns at other prehistoric sacred sites, such as Avebury (another early astronomical observatory): whirlpool shapes which he mapped carefully in his book, *The Pattern of the Past*,[20] but which he could not fully explain.*

Similar sacred sites in ancient China were found by use of the 'geomancer's compass', an instrument inscribed with the signs of the zodiac. As we'll see in a later chapter, this same instrument was also used in Chinese medical diagnosis.

All of which seems to point to some connection between the stars, Earth's magnetic forces, and the physiology of living creatures. Colin Wilson,[21] among others, suggests that the connection works something like this:

1. The solar system is permeated with fields of electromagnetic forces. Planetary movements change these fields.

2. Changes in these fields in turn affect the Earth's magnetic currents – just as changes in the Moon's tidal pull affect ocean currents.

3. These currents of Earth magnetism in turn affect the electrical 'life fields' of all living things.

Whether or not we agree completely with this strictly rational explanation of astrology, it seems to make sense even at the most basic level: Earth magnetism is caused by the rotation of the Earth, much as the magnetic field of a dynamo is produced by its spinning rotor. We can mark the Earth's rotation by the rising of certain constellations in the East – in other words, by the zodiac.

Ancient astrologers used the zodiac in just this way. On 1 January at midnight, they would have seen Libra rising; at 2 am, Scorpio rising, and so on, through all the twelve signs and the twenty-four hours. They would also have noticed radical differences between children born at different times on this 'zodiac clock': Those born with Libra rising would seem, on the whole, quiet and dreamy; those with Scorpio rising would seem far more active and boisterous, even in the cradle. Later in life, other differences would characterize the different types. In adolescence, for instance,

* Nor has anyone explained why Glastonbury and Stonehenge are each surrounded by earthworks and mounds tracing the shapes of giant zodiac figures (see Note 14, p. 213).

Librans would tend to have unusually clear complexions and to grow tall and slender; Scorpions would tend to show early sexual maturity and to grow muscular and stocky. Each of the twelve types would conform, in a general way, to a different, unique pattern of health and illness, body type and facial characteristics.

The rising sign, or *Ascendant*, is still a major factor in any birth chart. It is the basic indicator of general health and physical characteristics – the 'raw material' with which a person begins life. Often astrologers are able to guess a person's rising sign simply by looking at him, and sometimes the physical characteristics (build, height and even facial features) are quite marked. Naturally such characteristics also depend upon the genes – tall parents do not often have short offspring – but even brothers and sisters show the marks of their rising signs.

For example, someone born with Capricorn rising is said to be short and slender, with a long face, long nose, firm lips, a strong, narrow chin and a thin neck. Lobeless ears are common, so is thinning hair. Brows are often pointed.

The two Irish writers mentioned earlier, James Joyce and James Stephens, were both born the same day and hour, with Capricorn rising. Their photographs show both to have almost all of the above facial features, including long noses, narrow chins, thin necks, pointed eyebrows and lobeless ears. They look enough alike to be brothers.[22] Queen Elizabeth II, also born with Capricorn rising, has many of the above features, though her ears appear to have lobes.

Later, we'll see how the Ascendant works in the health horoscope in greater detail. First, here are the twelve signs of the zodiac again, with their traditional rulership over twelve regions of the body:

Symbol	Sign	Rules
♈	Aries, the Ram	the head
♉	Taurus, the Bull	the throat and neck
♊	Gemini, the Twins	the lungs and arms
♋	Cancer, the Crab	the stomach
♌	Leo, the Lion	the heart and spine
♍	Virgo, the Virgin	the abdomen and intestines

♎	Libra, the Scales	the kidneys
♏	Scorpio, the Scorpion	the reproductive organs
♐	Sagittarius, the Archer	the thighs and hips
♑	Capricorn, the Sea-Goat	the knees
♒	Aquarius, the Water-man	the lower legs, ankles
♓	Pisces, the Two Fish	the feet

In this way, the complete zodiac rules the complete body, literally from head to toe. But it is not just an arbitrary division of the body into twelve compartments. Zodiac signs are also divisions of *time* (a rising sign is two hours, a Sun sign is a month, etc). The list above makes sense in terms of the development of a child in the womb: The head forms first (third week), then the heartbeat appears (sixth week), then the limbs (eighth week) and finally the feet and toes (eleventh week). Thus the signs represent not only a spatial order, but also an organic and temporal order, outlining the essential development of the human body.

This order, the 'zodiac man', is the earliest and most important principle of bioastrology. Its discovery, thousands of years ago, placed human life within the living circle of cosmic forces, symbolized by the stone circles of the earliest observatories.

Today the 'zodiac man' gives a foundation for the health horoscope: If *a particular sign* is prominent in one person's birth chart, it indicates strength or weakness in *a particular part* of that person's body. The Geminian, for example, may be prone to bronchitis or other chest complaints. The Leo could, if his chart shows negative indications, have a weak heart.

Figure 1 shows the zodiac circle with all parts of the body and their ruling signs. Not only does each sign affect its own portion of the body, it also affects the portion opposite. Thus Aries affects not only the head, but the kidneys (ruled by Libra, opposite). This effect is called the *reflex* of a sign. Here are all the signs with their rules and reflexes:

Sign	*Rule*	*Reflex*
Aries	head	kidneys
Taurus	throat, neck	reproductive organs
Gemini	lungs, arms	thighs, hips

Cancer	stomach	knees
Leo	heart, spine	ankles, lower legs
Virgo	abdomen, intestines	feet
Libra	kidneys	head
Scorpio	reproductive organs	throat, neck
Sagittarius	thighs, hips	lungs, arms
Capricorn	knees	stomach
Aquarius	ankles, lower legs	heart, spine
Pisces	feet	abdomen, intestines

This means that anyone born with an ill-aspected planet in Aquarius may show a tendency to heart trouble. Knowing this, we are at last in a position to begin explaining the sudden heart attacks of Bing Crosby and Elvis Presley,

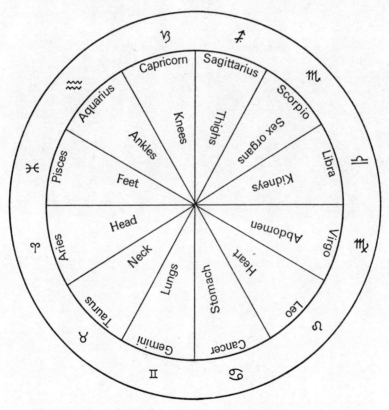

1. 'Zodiac man', showing the body region ruled by each sign.

mentioned on p. 9 above. Both men were born with Saturn (♄) ill-aspected in Aquarius; both men died with Saturn in Leo (see Figure 2).

Every birth chart contains all twelve zodiac signs. The actual effect of any particular sign depends on its 'prominence' in the chart. Usually a sign is called prominent if it is found in some critical position (eg, rising) or if it contains an important planet.* Chapter Two introduces the most important of the planets, the life-giving Sun.

* By convention, the word 'planet' in astrology includes not only the planets but the Sun and Moon.

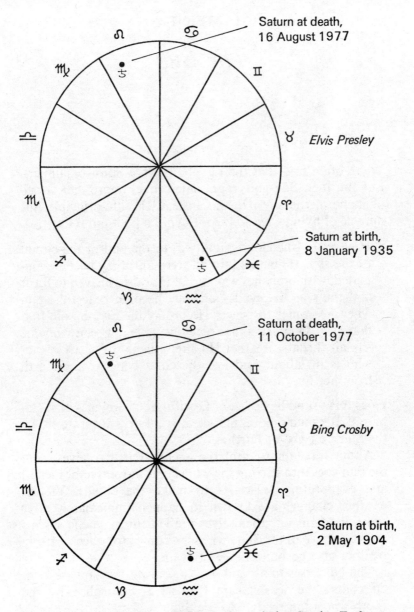

2. Saturn in the birth charts of Elvis Presley and Bing Crosby. Each was born with Saturn in Aquarius, and each died when Saturn had moved into the opposite sign, Leo. Leo is the ruler of the heart, and both men died of heart attacks.

27

CHAPTER TWO

The Sun

We're often told that the Egyptians were Sun-worshippers. But Rā, their Sun-god, represented much more than a ball of flame in the sky. He was instead the life-principle, the miracle of living Creation. An Egyptian poet put it like this:

> He lives in [the clouds, uplifted] to the end of the circuit of the sky. He enters into all trees and they become animated, with branches waving . . . He raises heaven to furor and the seas to revolt, and they become peaceful again when he comes to peace. He brings the divine Nile to a flood . . . One hears his voice but he is not seen while he lets all throats breathe. He strengthens the heart of her who is in labour and lets the child which comes forth from her live.[1]

Does this sound like a list of fanciful poetic images or metaphors? It's much more, in fact, it is a fairly accurate list of the Sun's effects on Earth:

About three-quarters of the energy Earth receives from the Sun goes into stirring the winds that move tree-branches, and evaporating sea-water to make the clouds. Violent weather changes are known to happen immediately after sunspots. Sunspots themselves are violent magnetic storms on the surface of the Sun; when 'he comes to peace', earthly weather also becomes peaceful again.

The Nile rises to a flood once a year, at the same season. Of course the seasons are themselves controlled by the Earth's position relative to the Sun.

'He lets all throats breathe' can only mean life-giving oxygen. All of the oxygen on our planet comes from vegetation, and all of the chemical energy in plants has been converted from solar energy. This Sun energy, through the plants, fuels all animal life on Earth, including the lives of the newborn children. Every calorie in everything we eat, from mothers' milk to the frozen, processed food at the supermarket, is ultimately a calorie of solar energy.

Energy is the key to Egyptian thoughts about the Sun. Their scientists were not so far from our scientists in many ways, though ours say it more prosaically: 'All life is maintained by the solar energy that is converted into chemical energy by plants. From the beginning of recorded history men recognized the life-giving role of the mysterious sun . . . The sun is hardly less mysterious today.'[2]

To our scientists, the Sun is a yellow dwarf star, mainly composed of hydrogen heated to an internal temperature of a million degrees Centigrade; the volume of the Sun is a million times that of Earth. Spectral analysis shows the Sun to be a giant alchemical furnace in which are dissolved all known elements. Its enormous energy of 10^{23} kilowatts (one, followed by twenty-three zeroes) blows out past the planets as a 'solar wind' of charged particles, as well as light and heat. The Sun might be said to be the central energy pump of the solar system: its heart.

The Egyptians associated the Sun directly with the human heart, as we can guess from the line 'He strengthens the heart . . .' They *knew*, in some mysterious way, a truth that we are only beginning to guess: The Sun can directly affect the heart.

On 17 May 1959 a magnetic storm rumbled across the face of the Sun, causing three spectacular (to astronomers) eruptions. At a hospital by the Black Sea that normally deals with two heart patients per day, this was a significant event: Next day, the hospital admitted twenty heart patients.[3] Two heart specialists in France have found a close correspondence between such solar activity and heart failure.[4] The rate of heart attacks in New England increases during years of heavy sunspot activity.[5] No one has yet explained the connection – at least no one in modern times.

The Egyptians may have found the answer by taking a larger view of man's relation to the cosmos. Their astrology was not concerned with omens or predictions, but with life: How to preserve it and how to extend it.

Egyptian medical science included the study of astrology, herbal remedies and surgery. Where medicine failed and death seemed inevitable, they tried preserving the body by mummification, against the day when they might once again restore the life force. Modern scientists are likewise attempting to freeze people cryogenically at death against the day when they hope to find the cure for what killed them – when they hope to restore the life force.

The Egyptians believed this life force to be Sun power, and they set about building a magnificent, mysterious instrument for collecting this power – the Great Pyramid.

This, one of the largest structures built by man, was designed by the astrologer-physician Imhotep. In shape, it is like a giant crystal of magnetite. Its placement is odd: set exactly one-third of the distance from the equator to the North Pole, and at the exact centre of all the land surface of the world. The 'tomb' inside it is equipped with observation shafts aimed at certain stars. It does not sound at all like a burial place for King Cheops – but it does sound like an instrument of astrology. John Michell, John Ivimy and others[6] have explained the numerous geometric similarities between the Pyramid and Stonehenge; it is at least possible that the two structures had a similar purpose.

While visiting the Pyramid's inner chambers a few years ago, M. Bovis found the bodies of a few small desert animals that had crept into this cool retreat and died. Their bodies were perfectly mummified. He suspected that the Pyramid *shape* might have somehow preserved them. At home he built a model of the Pyramid and placed a dead cat inside: It too mummified.

Biologist Lyall Watson repeated the test, using a cardboard pyramid and (as a 'control') an ordinary shoebox. Into each he placed fresh eggs and fresh meat. 'The ones in the pyramid kept quite well, while those in the box soon began to smell and had to be thrown out. I am forced to conclude that a cardboard model of the Cheops pyramid is not just a random arrangement of pieces of paper, but does

30

have special properties.'[7] Since decay is caused by bacteria, the effect of the pyramid shape must be to kill these bacteria, or at least retard their growth.

It is now known that container shapes can have real effects on life processes. The bacteria that make yoghurt are able to work faster in one special shape of container – and that shape has been patented. Czech brewers recently tried putting beer into square barrels, and found that it soured – bacterial action again. In Germany, the healing of wounds has been speeded up by enclosing them in spherical chambers.[8]

As biologists know, a life process can only be hastened or retarded by adding or subtracting energy. If shapes affect life processes, they must do so by somehow altering energy fields. The pyramid shape, for instance, could prevent decay by focusing solar energy in some way. Just how a cardboard pyramid can preserve fresh meat and eggs is not clear, but it does.

What is clear is that the traditional shapes of solar instruments like Stonehenge and the Pyramid were not accidental; these shapes are inherent in the structure of the zodiac.

The circle of Stonehenge represents the *ecliptic*, the yearly path of the Sun as it passes through the twelve signs. Of course the Sun does not actually move, but the earth's orbit around it gives the Sun an apparent motion which can be mapped against the distant stars. At the first moment of spring, the Sun stands at 0° of Aries, and it moves nearly a degree per day. Since each sign has 30 degrees, the Sun takes just over thirty days to transit each sign; it completes the entire circle (360°) in exactly a year.

As we saw at the beginning of Chapter One, your Sun sign is a clue to your character. It is also a clue to your probable state of health. The character and health indications for each Sun sign are given in Part Two below, but let's anticipate this with one example:

Taurus produces 'a quiet, home-loving person, with a down-to-earth, practical nature . . . comfortable to be with, and certainly the most easy-going of friends'. Since Taurus rules the throat, 'Taureans commonly suffer from throat infections, goitre, asthma, sinus infections, neuralgia in neck muscles, ear infections and dental problems (usually of the lower jaw).' But 'Taurean resistance to infection is normally good . . .', and many of those born under this sign can expect reasonably good health. The fact that Taurus rules the throat can of course work favourably, too: Taurus produces singers. If we try to think of a quiet, easy-going, home-loving singer, Bing Crosby once more comes to mind, and so does Perry Como. Both were born with the Sun in Taurus.

Not everyone fits his Sun sign so perfectly, running true to type. But the fact that there are twelve distinct types is itself puzzling – what's so special about twelve? Seeking the answer leads us once more to the structure of the zodiac.

While the early astronomers of Britain built circular observatories, those of Babylon built square ones, called *ziggurats*. This reminds us that the year is not only a solar circle, but divided also into four seasons. If we inscribe a square in the zodiac circle (Figure 3) it marks the four signs which begin the seasons: Aries begins the spring on 21 March; Cancer begins the summer on 22 June; Libra the autumn on 23 September; Capricorn the winter on 22 December. These four are called the *Cardinal* ('hinge') signs, since they mark the year's four turning points. Those born in the Cardinal signs are said to be given to quick action and spontaneity: They are decisive, but sometimes hasty.

Another square connects the next four signs (Taurus, Leo, Scorpio and Aquarius) which lie at the middle of each season. They are the *Fixed* signs, thought to signify firmness and deliberate action, thoroughness and endurance, but sometimes stubbornness.

A third square connects the remaining four signs (Gemini, Virgo, Sagittarius and Pisces) each of which marks the dwindling of its season. These are the *Mutable* ('changing') signs, and by tradition they give flexibility and indecisive action. Persons born in these signs tend to be open-minded, but also sometimes tend to dither.

These sets of four signs are called the quadruplicities. They give us part of the picture for each sign. They explain

in part why the Arien is quick, 'rambunctious', and sometimes accident-prone; why the Taurean is quiet and un-
flappable; and why the Geminian is vacillating and nervous.
But it does not explain why Taureans and Leos (both born
under Fixed signs) are very different.

The next stage in the evolution of early observatories is

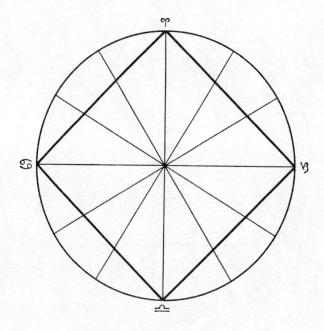

3. The square of Cardinal signs, marking the four seasons, which begin
with Aries (March 21), Cancer (June 22), Libra (September 23), and
Capricorn (December 22).

the Pyramid. Its triangular side represents another logical
division of the zodiac: the triplicities. If we inscribe a triangle on zodiac circle (Figure 4) it connects the three *Fire*
signs (Aries, Leo and Sagittarius). Those born under the
Fire signs are known for zeal and enthusiasm, fiery energy
and an urge to plunge into any task headfirst.

Another triangle connects the three *Earth* signs (Taurus,

Virgo and Capricorn). Earth-people are usually constructive and practical, known for their common sense.

A third triangle connects the three *Air* signs (Gemini, Libra and Aquarius). Those born in Air signs have an airy, changeable nature; they are likeable and communicative.

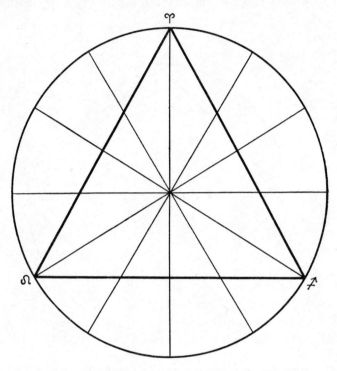

4. The triangle of Fire signs: Aries, Leo, Sagittarius.

Finally a triangle connects the three *Water* signs (Cancer, Scorpio and Pisces). Those born in Water signs are generally deeply emotional persons; their emotionality can manifest itself as thin-skinned sensitivity, or as sympathy and understanding.

The authors of *The Case for Astrology* suggest that Fire, Earth, Air and Water, which are the four traditional elements of alchemy, may also represent the four chemical elements found in all living creatures: Hydrogen, Carbon, Oxygen and Nitrogen.[9] In any case, there are four triplicities, just as there are four triangular sides to a pyramid, and they do represent four well-known sides to human character. Our language is full of expressions like 'down-to-earth', 'watery sentiment', 'blowing with the wind' and 'a real ball of fire'.

Together, the quadruplicities and the triplicities define the zodiac. We now see how Taureans and Leos are both firm and deliberate in their actions (both being Fixed signs), but how they differ: Taureans are known for earthy common sense; Leos for fiery enthusiasm.

There remains one more division of the zodiac, and that is the simplest possible: the polarities. All ancient religions recognized the fundamental duality of the universe, and of human nature. The idea of male and female, positive/negative, Yin/Yang is embedded in our way of thinking about the world. The zodiac takes account of this, having six *positive* signs alternating with six *negative* signs.

The positive signs (Aries, Gemini, Leo, Libra, Sagittarius and Aquarius) tend to produce people who are active, extraverted and rational. The negative signs (Taurus, Cancer, Virgo, Scorpio, Capricorn and Pisces) tend to produce people who are passive, introverted and intuitive.

The Egyptians represented these polarities by the Sun and Moon, which they called 'the right and left eyes of Heaven'. By tradition, astrology has always characterized these two luminaries in this way:

Sun	*Moon*
positive	negative
masculine	feminine
life-giving	life-bearing
active	passive
rational	intuitive
obvious, open	mysterious, occult
thought	dream
extravert	introvert

In physiological terms, the Sun seems to correspond to the left brain hemisphere (which controls the right side of the body) and in most people, this hemisphere is dominant.

Neurologists find that it controls speech, reason and mathematical thinking.

The Moon corresponds to the right brain hemisphere (left side of the body), which is receptive. Neurologists find that this brain hemisphere controls subtle, intuitive thinking, and

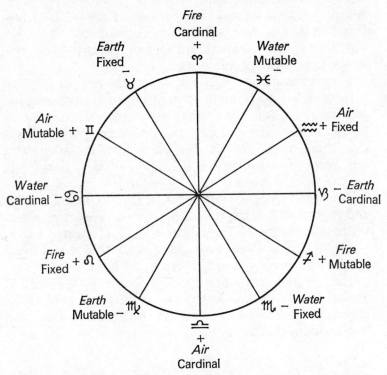

5. The pattern of the zodiac. Each sign represents a different combination of the four elements (Earth, Air, Fire and Water), the three seasonal qualities (Cardinal, Fixed and Mutable), and the two polarities (Masculine and Feminine), marked with plus and minus signs.

appreciation of music, and that it is a source of dream and memory.

Figure 5 shows the complete zodiac structure, with quadruplicities, triplicities and polarities.

Early in 1977 Professor H. J. Eysenck of the Institute of Psychiatry in London announced a new and convincing test of some of these principles. He cooperated with the astrologer Jeff Mayo in obtaining the horoscopes of 2400 persons. These persons were asked to complete a standard psychological test measuring neuroticism and also extraversion. The test scores were compared to their Sun signs.

We might expect neuroticism to equate with the astrological term 'emotionality'. Those born with the Sun in a Water sign (Cancer, Scorpio or Pisces) should score higher than others. The test showed that neuroticism was indeed higher in these three emotional signs that in any others.

Extraversion should be high in positive signs, low in negative signs. Again, this is exactly how the test turned out.[10] It begins to look as if modern science is at last beginning to prove (or re-prove) some of the fundamental truths known to the astrologers of ancient Egypt and used in astrology ever since.

CHAPTER THREE

The Moon

On 19 June 1943 one of the largest race riots in US history broke out in Detroit. Twenty-four years were to pass before Detroit experienced another such outbreak of mass hysteria: On 23 July 1967 race riots flared up in Detroit and four other cities. On both occasions there was a Full Moon.

The Full Moon does seem to trigger irrational, 'lunatic' behaviour, such as riots and uprisings. The Russian revolution started at Full Moon in March 1917 (February by the old Russian Calendar), and so did the Hungarian uprising of October 1956. These and many other Full Moon 'coincidences' may baffle psychologists and historians, but they are no surprise to astrologers. In astrology the Moon has long been associated with deep instinctual drives and sudden emotional changes – in other words, with the subconscious.

The first astrologers to make a systematic study of the Moon were the Babylonians (or, as the Greeks called them, the Chaldeans). About 4000 BC they began keeping careful day-to-day records of almost everything that happened in the sky – the appearance of the Moon, the erratic movements of the planets, the rising and setting of familiar constellations, and even the appearance of new stars.*

The Babylonians considered the Moon the most important of the seven planets. They studied it intensively, keeping careful records of lunar phases, eclipses, and the position

* About 4000 BC they recorded a bright new star, or supernova (see *Scientific American*, July 1976, p. 66). We cannot say why they found it important, but a medical researcher writes: 'There is some evidence that supernovae can be a factor in epidemic diseases...' (G. Maxwell Cade, in *New Scientist*, 19 September 1968). We do know that the Babylonians used astrology to predict epidemics and other events of national importance.

of the Moon in the zodiac from day to day. Lunar cycles were calculated with amazing accuracy: For example, the astrologer Kidinnu found the lengths of the four types of month,* each to within less than a second of time, without using clocks, calculators or even numerical fractions. His results can still be used by astronomers.

Careful records and accuracy were necessary, because the Moon is the fastest-moving object in the sky. While the Sun remains in one sign for about thirty days, the Moon remains only about two days. Lunar influence thus changes constantly, showing effects that appear and pass off quickly.

The Moon appears to affect us in three ways: Through the environment, through the body, and through the mind.

1. *Lunar influence on the environment.* Obviously the tidal force of the Moon affects submarine plant and animal life. Dr Frank A. Brown of Northwestern University found that oysters open their shells when the Moon passes directly overhead. This is true not only of oysters in the ocean, but of oysters kept in a tank of water in Illinois – a thousand miles from the ocean. These simple molluscs, and many other creatures, can somehow detect the faint gravitational force of the Moon passing overhead.[1]

In fact there is a tidal force in every body of water, even in a dewdrop. The liquid within every cell of the human body undergoes a slight change under the pull of lunar gravity. And of course there is also a lunar tide in the amniotic fluid of the womb – the environment in which we spend our first nine months of life.

The Moon also affects our postnatal environment, namely our weather, according to two articles in one issue of *Science* magazine. One article surveyed weather reports over a

---

* These are:

The *synodical* month, the time from one New Moon to the next = 29 days 12 hours 44 min 2·9 sec;

The *sidereal* month, the actual time it takes the Moon to orbit the Earth = 27 days 7 hours 43 min 11·5 sec;

The *anomalistic* month, the cycle of the Moon's closest approach to the Earth = 27 days 13 hours 18 min 39·3 sec; and

The *eclipse* month, the cycle of the Moon's crossing of the Sun's path = 27 days 5 hours 5 min 36 sec.

period of forty-nine years in North America; the other, weather reports over twenty-five years in Australia. Both concluded that heavy rains occur more often three to four days after Full Moon than at any other time of month.[2]

Lunar influence over tides and rainfall suggests that the Moon has an essentially 'watery' nature, and this has long been recognized by astrologers. Just as the Sun rules radiant, warm Leo (a Fire sign), so the Moon rules cool, self-contained Cancer (a Water Sign).

2. *Lunar influence on the body.* The Moon appears to control the flow of body fluids, including blood. A Tennessee surgeon, Dr Edson Andrews, found that haemorrhaging during operations occurs most frequently at Full Moon. His survey of 1000 patients with haemorrhages showed that '82 per cent of all the bleeding crises occurred between the first and last quarters of the moon, with a significant peak when the moon was full'.[3]

The menstrual cycle is likewise subject to lunar influence. An American Air Force physicist, Dr E. M. Dewan, discovered that the *light* of the Full Moon can influence ovulation. This is not to say that all women ovulate at Full Moon. But Nature seems to have provided women with a sensitive biological clock, attuned to a lunar cycle of approximately twenty-eight days. In natural surroundings, the light of the Full Moon would serve as a time-marker, to adjust and regulate this clock. There is evidence that many animal fertility cycles work this way and, in Dr Dewan's view, the Full Moon was the ancestral regulator for the human fertility cycle. He suggested that many women now having irregular periods have had this clock disturbed by artificial lighting: 'To test this remarkable idea . . . he arranged for twenty women to leave the light on in their bedrooms for three nights commencing on the fourteenth day after menstruation. The results were dramatic, with all women regularizing their menstrual cycle.'[4] That the Moon has power over fertility and childbirth is an idea as old as Babylon. In Chapter Two we saw how the Egyptians gave the Sun an important role in childbirth. There is actually no conflict between these two views: The Sun represents the male, active, life-giving principle, because it radiates energy. The Moon represents the female, passive, life-bearing principle because it reflects and transmutes that energy, as moonlight. Neither planet is all-important: what is important is the relation between them.

At Full Moon the Sun and Moon must be in opposite

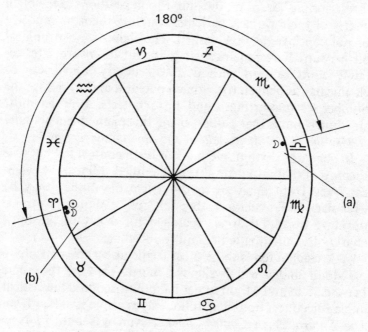

6. Sun and Moon in opposition (a) and conjunction (b).

parts of the zodiac (as seen from Earth). Astrologers say they are in *opposition* (see Figure 6a). If they are in *perfect* opposition, the Earth's shadow crosses the Moon and we have a lunar eclipse. But usually the term 'opposition' applied to the Sun and Moon simply means Full Moon.

At New Moon the Sun and Moon must be in the same part of the zodiac, and astrologers then say they are in *conjunction* (see Figure 6b). If the conjunction is perfect, the Moon passes in front of the Sun for a solar eclipse. But usually a conjunction of the Sun and Moon simply means New Moon.

Obviously the Sun and Moon can be at any angle from each other, from 0° (conjunction) to 180° (opposition). And these Sun–Moon angles are of primary importance in a theory called 'astrological birth control'.

For some years, the Czech doctor Eugen Jonas and the group of physicians who work with him have been issuing 'prescriptions' based on the Sun–Moon positions in the birth charts of their women patients, enabling them to conceive or not conceive, as they wished. The claims for astrological birth control are remarkable: It is said to ensure safe, reliable contraception without pills, surgery, appliances or chemicals; to help sterile women ovulate; and to reduce the number of miscarriages and birth defects. But the most startling claim is that parents using this method can actually *choose the sex of their child at the time of conception.*[5]

In general, 'rhythm' methods of birth control fail because the day of ovulation cannot be identified. Menstrual cycles can vary from nineteen to thirty-five days; they may be irregular, and ovulation may take place more than once during a cycle. Dr Jonas searched for a key in the birth charts of women patients, and found that:

a. A woman tends to be most fertile at exactly that phase of Moon under which she was born. That is, the angle between Sun and Moon in her natal horoscope is the critical angle for conception. The following example is taken from *The Natural Birth Control Book*:[6] Ann was born in New York City between 1 and 3 am on 14 November 1927. At that moment the Moon was 247° from the Sun. Whenever the Sun and Moon are again at this angle, she will be at the end of a fertile period. Adding a safety factor of 6 degrees, she obtains a 'working angle' of 253°.

Knowing this, it is possible for Ann to work out (using Moon tables) her fertile and infertile times for any month: Fertility begins exactly four days before the angle reaches 253° and ends at 253°. Figure 7a shows the Sun and Moon in Ann's birth chart, and Figure 7b shows her fertile time for the month of June 1977.

Dr Jonas tested this method with 1252 patients over a year, and found that it worked on 98 per cent of them –

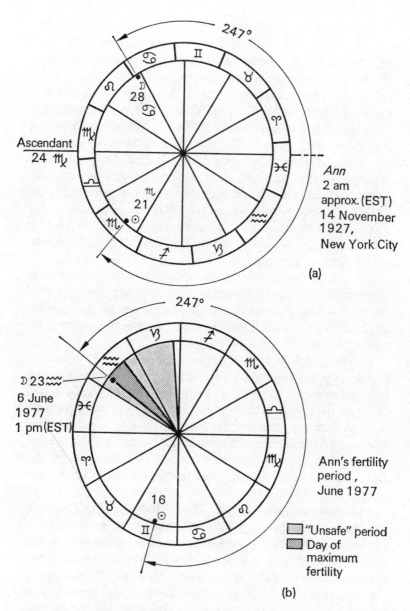

7. Sun, Moon and fertility. The Sun–Moon angle at a woman's birth (a) is duplicated once a month. According to the Jonas theory, this angle marks the end of the period of maximum fertility for that month (b) (the black area).

43

making it about as reliable as the Pill.[7]

b. The sex of a child depends upon whether, at the time of conception, the Moon is in a positive or negative sign. When the Moon is in a positive sign (Aries, Gemini, Leo, Libra, Sagittarius or Aquarius), the child will be male; a negative sign (Taurus, Cancer, Virgo, Scorpio, Capricorn or Pisces) will produce a female child: 'At the Bratislava clinic [of Gynaecology] he worked out the individual calculations for eight thousand women who wanted to have boys. Ninety-five per cent got their made-to-order boy.'[8] Continuing the example of Ann of New York, assume that she wishes to conceive a child in July 1977, and hopes for a girl. The time favourable for conception in July 1977 is 5 and 6 July. As Figure 8 shows, during this entire time, the Moon is in Pisces, a 'girl-sign'.[9]

c. The risk of conceiving unhealthy or deformed children is greater for certain women, namely those born at Full Moon. Dr Jonas warns that women with a natal Sun–Moon angle of 180° 'must take care not to conceive when this pattern recurs'.[10]

The Full Moon is clearly associated with crises in human physiology. It even seems to be associated with that greatest of crises in every human life: birth. Drs W. and A. Menaker checked over half a million births in New York hospitals, finding that the greatest number occur just after the Full Moon, and the least number occur just after the New Moon. A study from North Germany seems to confirm this cycle.[11] But the Full Moon is also associated with crises of the human mind.

3. *Lunar influence on the mind.* 'Moon-madness' sounds like pure superstition. There is a persistent recurrence of headlines like these: LUNAR MADMAN ON THE PROWL AGAIN (from Bath, Somerset); MAD HEADHUNTER OF PLAINFIELD STRIKES AGAIN IN FULL MOON (from Plainfield, Wisconsin).[12] Agreed, these might be prompted by editorial hysteria, but why should editors or anyone else link the Full Moon with madness?

The fact is that the staff of mental hospitals find certain of their patients becoming more violent at Full Moon.

44

Crimes of rape, vandalism and insane murder tend to increase at Full Moon and decrease at New Moon. According to Joseph Goodavage, 'racial rioting always reaches a peak of frenzy during Full Moon periods',[13] and we've already seen examples of this.

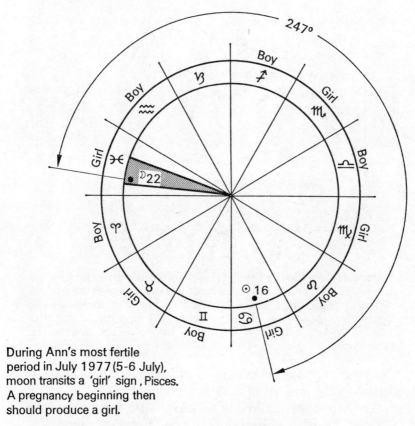

During Ann's most fertile period in July 1977 (5-6 July), moon transits a 'girl' sign, Pisces. A pregnancy beginning then should produce a girl.

8. Choosing a child's sex at conception. The shaded area shows Ann's period of maximum fertility for July 1977. Since the entire area lies within the 'feminine' sign Pisces, a child conceived at this time will be a girl.

Both the American Institute of Medical Climatology and the Philadelphia Police Department have published reports showing that psychotic crimes – including arson, destructive driving, kleptomania and homicidal alcoholism – are most frequent at Full Moon, while well motivated crimes such as robbery and fraud remain at a steady level throughout the month.[14] The same link between the Full Moon and criminal psychosis can be seen in Britain, as Figure 9 demonstrates.

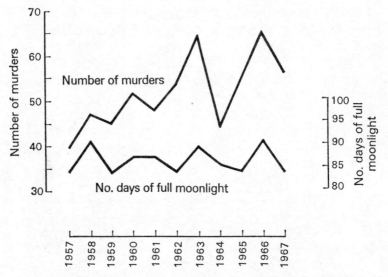

9. Murder by moonlight? Top line shows abnormal murders for England and Wales, 1957–1967: those murders for which criminals were found insane, or guilty of manslaughter with 'diminished responsibility'. Bottom line shows days of full moonlight (3½ days before and after each Full Moon) for same years. The two lines match for nine out of the twelve years.

Nearly every peak in the number of insane murders matches a peak in the number of days of full moonlight.

The Moon was full on 20 February 1946, when one such 'lunatic' struck in Texarkana, Texas. Finding a man and woman parked in Lover's Lane, he beat both of them unconscious and raped the woman. The next Full Moon was 24 March, when he attacked another couple, this time mutilating the woman with a knife and blowing the man's brains out. The next was on 13 April, when the killer found another parked couple, shot the man three times through the head, then dragged the woman into the woods where he raped and murdered her. On 3 May he shot at a couple

46

through the window of their home. Shortly after this an unidentified man threw himself under a train, and the series of murders came to an end.

The Los Angeles burglar-rapist Clinton DeWitt Cook was likewise seized by uncontrollable violent sexual urges at the Full Moon. For ten months in 1939–40 he broke into a series of houses to terrorize single women students and baby-sitters, raping and beating all of them, and murdering one. According to Colin Wilson, a lunar cycle can be found in the notorious 'lipstick murders' of William Hierens in Chicago, and in the crimes of Jack the Ripper.[15]

Dr Leonard J. Ravitz, a neurologist and psychiatric consultant at Duke University, has for some years been studying the variations in body electricity, or 'biopotential' in both normal persons and mental patients. Biopotential seems to be a measure of emotional disturbance: a high reading indicates emotional upset.

Dr Ravitz found that the highest readings (in everyone) occur at Full Moon. The more severely disturbed the patient, the greater the effect, but everyone seems to become more unstable during this key Moon phase.[16]

The Moon's association with the deeper levels of the unconscious mind is not always so negative. Inspirations, dreams, subtle truths arrived at by pure intuition – these too belong to the Moon. Moon-goddesses have long been the patronesses of poets and mystics the world over. The scholar and poet Robert Graves wrote *The White Goddess* in an attempt to trace the myths of Greece, Babylon, India, Europe, Africa – the myths of virtually all known cultures of the past – to a central source. He came up with the conclusion that the earliest source of all inspiration is the 'Lunar Muse'.

Artists and scientists alike understand what sudden insight can mean – but so can anyone who has ever tackled any difficult problem (even an intractable crossword clue). One struggles with it, gives up, and then suddenly from the depths of the unconscious mind, the answer flashes into view. The biographies of scientists are filled with such stories: Archimedes is relaxing in his bath when ('Eureka!') he

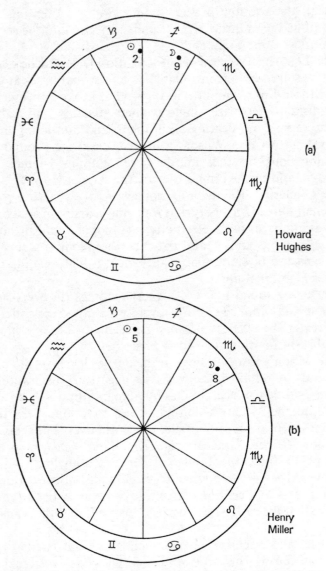

10. Horoscopes for Howard Hughes and Henry Miller, showing only Sun and Moon positions. (a) Howard Hughes, born 24 December 1905, has the Sun in Capricorn, a sign of ambition, and the Moon in Sagittarius, a sign of foresight. (b) Henry Miller, born 26 December 1891, also has the Sun in Capricorn, but the Moon in Scorpio, a sign of deep sexuality.

invents the true test for the density of gold. August Kekule is taking a nap (and dreaming of primordial alchemical symbols) when he awakes with the answer to the structure of the benzene molecule. Riding on a bus, the mathematician Poincaré suddenly finds the answer to a difficult major problem. He *knows* it is the answer at once, though it takes him years of hard work to prove it.

There seems no way of proving that the Moon has an effect on inspirations of this kind, but it does seem to stir man's subconscious depths, bringing mythic truth to the surface. Robert Graves kept some African art objects on his desk while writing *The White Goddess*; only later did he learn that these objects – from different parts of Africa, and given him by different friends – were all fetishes of the Moon-goddess. The first two publishers who saw his book rejected it. Both died shortly thereafter, one of heart disease, the other committed suicide. The third publisher accepted it, and was shortly to receive the Order of Merit. Coincidence? Graves writes: 'Chains of more-than-coincidence occur so often in my life that, if I am forbidden to call them supernatural hauntings, let me call them a habit. Not that I like the word "supernatural"; I find these happenings natural enough, though superlatively unscientific.'[17]

Yet the Moon seems to have had some effect on scientific history. In 1664 Isaac Newton fell ill with a kind of 'brain fever', a result of his excessive studies of the Moon. He therefore retired to the country, to recuperate. By so doing, he was doubly blessed: He missed the Great Plague of 1665 which made London a tomb, and he made the three major discoveries for which he is now famous: universal gravitation, the calculus, and the divisibility of white light into all the colours. He was then not yet twenty-five years old, and though he worked another sixty years, polishing and perfecting his ideas, he was never to make another great discovery.

This chapter can only give a hint of the complex influence of the Moon over the human body and mind. In Chapter Four, we'll see why the Moon sign alone is not enough to define the health outlook for any horoscope – just as the Sun sign or Rising sign alone is not enough.

Nevertheless, the Moon sign can make a considerable difference in personalities. If we compare two famous persons, both born with the Sun in Capricorn but with different Moon signs, the difference may be clearer. Figure 10a shows the partial birth chart of billionaire Howard Hughes, with the Sun in 2 degrees of Capricorn and the Moon in 9 degrees of Sagittarius. The main feature of lunar Sagittarians is their almost uncanny knack of foreseeing the future; since Capricornians are often ambitious and businesslike, it makes sense for such a person to make money out of his predictions – as Hughes made money out of predicting the future of commercial aviation.

Figure 10b shows the partial birth chart of Henry Miller, born with the Sun in 5 degrees of Capricorn and the Moon in 8 degrees of Scorpio. The lunar Scorpion may have a great deal of personal magnetism, combined with pride and stubbornness, but he could also be preoccupied with sex.

CHAPTER FOUR

Planet Rhythms

The Sun, Moon and Rising signs in the birth chart give only a general outline of someone's character or health. Details can be supplied only by a close study of the rest of the planets: their positions in the zodiac and relative to each other.

Here is a short key to the influences of all the planets:

	Planet	General influence	Influence on the body
☉	Sun	Power, self-expression	Vitality, heart, spine
☽	Moon	Intuition, change, inspiration	Nutrition, digestion, body fluids
☿	Mercury	Communication, intellect	Lungs, nervous system
♀	Venus	Harmony, love	Throat, kidneys, hormones
♂	Mars	Energy, aggression	Fever, red blood corpuscles, muscles
♃	Jupiter	Expansion, creativity	Health, growth, the liver
♄	Saturn	Contraction, conservation	Illness, ageing, blockages, the bones
♅	*Uranus*	Sudden change, electromagnetism	Circulation, body electricity
♆	*Neptune*	Uncertainty	Effects of drugs, poisons
♇	*Pluto*	Earth forces (?)	Elimination, regeneration (?)

The influences of the last three planets, all discovered during the past two hundred years, are not yet completely determined. This is partly because these very distant, slow-moving planets take many years to transit a single sign.

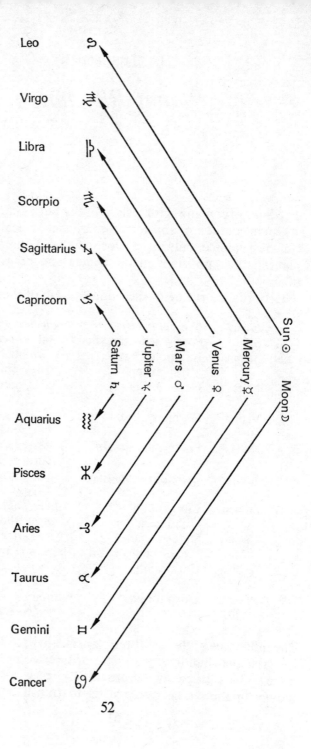

11. Planet rulership of the signs.

For example, Pluto, discovered in 1930, moves only about two degrees in one year, taking about fifteen years to transit each sign. For this reason, it's wise not to place too much emphasis on the positions of Uranus, Neptune and Pluto; their indications are far weaker than those of the other planets.

Traditionally, the Sun rules Leo and the Moon rules Cancer, while each of the other planets rules two zodiac signs. The traditional scheme is shown in Figure 11. In modern times the three 'new' planets have been introduced into the scheme provisionally: Uranus rules Aquarius, Neptune rules Pisces, and Pluto rules Scorpio. Astrologers generally consider a planet's influence stronger when it is in its 'own' sign. For example, a person born with Jupiter (planet of growth, expansion) in Sagittarius (sign of the hips and thighs) is likely to show a tendency to put on weight around the hips.

The above short key is not meant to be a complete description of the influences of the planets (a far more comprehensive key is given on pp. 145–157 below), but if we combine it with the *zodiac man*, it is possible to see how horoscope diagnosis works:

Mercury, for example, rules the lungs and nervous system. Mercury in *Aries* (associated with the head) might therefore indicate some nerve difficulty in that region, such as neuralgia, shooting pains or numbness in the head or face, or dizziness. Mercury in *Taurus* (the throat region) might indicate nervous speech difficulties, such as a stammer. Mercury in *Gemini* (chest, arms) might indicate bronchial disorders or asthma. So through all the signs, Mercury would indicate nerve or lung problems.

Mars, on the other hand, would be associated with fevers, muscular aches, or injuries (wounds) in these same parts. For each of the planets, the planet itself indicates the nature of a possible problem, while the sign indicates that part of the body where the problem is manifested.

Saturn, believed by many to be a specific indicator of disease, is called a *malefic* planet. It represents contraction, constriction and physical blockages. In Virgo, Saturn could indicate blockages of the intestines (eg, constipation, colitis). In Aquarius (the lower legs, ankles) Saturn gives two main indications: First, since it means contraction and refers to the bones, it could indicate weak ankles. Secondly, it could indicate blockage of the blood vessels in the lower legs, known as thrombosis. Thrombosis is the condition brought about by a blood clot, often in the lower leg area; if the clot moves to the heart, it can bring about a heart attack.

As we saw at the beginning of this book, Bing Crosby and Elvis Presley were both born with Saturn ill-aspected in Aquarius, and both died of heart attacks. We cannot say whether their attacks had identical or even similar causes, but the double coincidence does point out one fact: *How you live is just as important as your stars.* Both men's charts bore the same warning indication, yet they died at very different ages. By living in a sensible, relaxed, unstressful manner, by playing golf and keeping generally fit, Bing Crosby managed to live seventy-three years. Elvis Presley, who drove himself hard, and perhaps took medication to keep going, succumbed at the age of forty-two.

Not everyone with Saturn in Aquarius is a candidate for a heart attack, of course, so it may be worth while to consider the birth chart of the apparently very healthy Shirley MacLaine (Figure 12). Miss MacLaine's chart shows a number of points of comparison with that of Bing Crosby:

1. Both were born with the Sun in Taurus. Taurean singers are quite common, because Taurus rules the throat, and because this sign is governed by Venus, the planet of beauty and harmony.

2. Both were born with Mars in Taurus, *conjunct* (close to) the Sun. This could point to a general tendency to throat infections, tonsillitis, etc.

3. Both were born with Saturn in Aquarius. In the case of Bing Crosby, Saturn is at an angle of about 90 degrees from the Sun and Mars (also Mercury). This is called a *square* aspect, and is usually thought to indicate trouble, possibly heart trouble.

In the birth chart of Shirley MacLaine, by contrast, Saturn is not in square with any planet. The malefic influence of Saturn cannot be expected to bring about any serious trouble. There is, however, some chance of weak ankles. While in her teens, and dancing in a ballet of *Cinderella*, Miss MacLaine actually broke an ankle: 'Practising some *grands jetés* before the show she stumbled and one of her never strong ankles folded under her and quietly snapped.'[1]

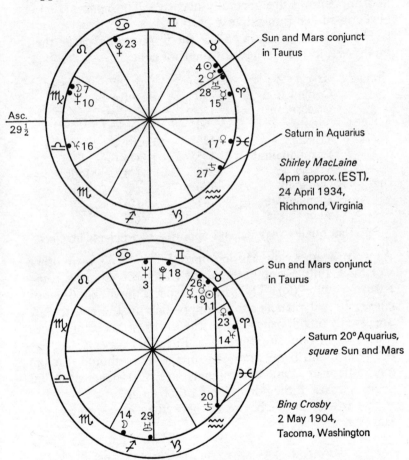

12. Horoscopes for Shirley MacLaine and Bing Crosby. Both have Saturn in Aquarius and a Mars–Sun conjunction in Taurus. In Ms MacLaine's chart (a) no aspect is formed. In Mr Crosby's chart (b), however, Saturn squares the Sun and Mars to warn of a serious health hazard, possibly affecting the heart.

55

The contrast between the birth charts of Shirley MacLaine and Bing Crosby illustrates the importance of 'aspects', the angular relationship between planets in the horoscope. Certain specific angles between planets are said to combine planetary influences either in a positive or a negative way. In Chapter Three we saw the *conjunction* (0°) and *opposition* (180°) of Sun and Moon; conjunctions are generally positive and oppositions are generally negative. The *square* (90°) is also considered a negative aspect.

The table below shows all of the important aspects, their qualities and the strength of their influence.

Symbol	Aspect	Angle	Quality*	Influence
☌	Conjunction	0°	Positive	
☍	Opposition	180°	Negative	Strong
□	Square	90°	Negative	
△	Trine	120°	Positive	
⌓	Sesquiquadrate	135°	(*)	
⚹	Sextile	60°	(*)	Moderate
⚻	Quincunx	150°	(*)	
∟	Semi-square	45°	(*)	Weak
⎯	Semi-sextile	30°	(*)	

* Actual quality may depend upon the two planets involved.

As we've seen, a Sun–Moon opposition (☉ ☍ ☽), or in other words, a Full Moon, is a negative aspect; so is a Sun–Saturn square (☉ □ ♄). Some aspects have an obvious cause: If two planets are in opposition in the chart, they are usually on opposite sides of the Earth, so their influences must pull in opposite directions. But other aspects, such as the square and trine, are not so plain. Why should it make any difference that two planets are 120 degrees or 90 degrees apart, rather than some other angle?

The answer to this begins in the Pythagorean principle of Harmony.

PYTHAGORAS AND THE RHYTHMS OF LIFE

In a sense, every doctor in the world is a member of the ancient and mystical Pythagorean Brotherhood. In the Hippocratic oath, a modern doctor swears allegiance to the humane principles laid down by the Brotherhood; Hippocrates, the father of modern medicine, was one of its most illustrious members.

The oath states that a doctor shall not kill, either wilfully or by neglect, that he shall treat patients without regard to his fee, and that he shall use his utmost skill and science to relieve pain and help Nature to effect a cure. According to *A Short History of Medicine*, the oath can be traced directly to the teachings of Pythagoras.[2]

Of Pythagoras himself we know little. He was born about 569 BC on the island of Samos, travelled to Egypt and Babylon to study, and finally formed his Brotherhood at Crotona, Italy, dedicated to the study of all natural mysteries. Healing was only a part of this study, for the Pythagoreans conceived of all Nature as guided by a single, universal principle which they called by a new name, *Armonia*, or 'harmony'. (A new name was needed also for this grand scheme of study; they called it 'philosophy'.)

Literally, harmony meant 'the way things fit together', and the first Pythagorean discovery was of the way music and mathematics fit together, in a surprisingly simple way. Taking a string tuned to emit a certain note (say middle C) when plucked, Pythagoras found that dividing the length in half, produces the note C again, one octave higher. In fact, the lengths $\frac{1}{2}, \frac{1}{3}, \frac{1}{4}, \frac{1}{5}, \frac{1}{6}$ and so on produce higher and higher versions of the same note C.

Harmony (in the musical sense) obeys another simple mathematical rule. Two strings produce harmonious ('sweet') chords when their lengths are in these proportions: $\frac{2}{3}, \frac{3}{4}, \frac{4}{5}, \frac{5}{6}, \frac{6}{7}$ and so on.

These proportions apply not only to plucked strings, but to all musical instruments: the spacing of holes in a flute, the length of tubing in a horn or organ pipe, the diameter of a bell. Every musical instrument has its own natural rate of vibration, or 'fundamental note'. What's more important, the same principle applies to other objects – in fact, to every object in the universe. One can make a wine glass ring, emitting sound energy at a certain pitch. If sound of the same pitch is put back into the glass (say, a note sung by a soprano), it will begin to vibrate until it shatters.

Waves of energy – sound, light, heat or electromagnetism – are constantly given off and constantly absorbed by every object in the universe, from atoms to entire galaxies. This is indeed a unifying principle of Nature, and Pythagoras was right to see it as the basic link between man and the cosmos.

The basic wave form of all energy transmission is shown in Figure 13. In the first half of the cycle, the energy increases to a maximum (positive) level, then declines. In the second half, it decreases to a minimum (negative) level, then rises. When it reaches 0, the cycle is ready to begin again. This too is mathematics, for, as cybernetician Dr David Foster has pointed out, it is a 'binary' system, the simplest element in the vocabulary of computers. Colin Wilson adds 'if we think of "waves" as the basic vocabulary of the universe, then you can think of life – in fact, of all matter – as being due to waves that have somehow been cybernetically programmed.'[3]

The human body responds to all types of energy. Industrial doctors are presently concerned about the possible effects of infrasound – sound frequencies generated by machinery, and too low to be heard. Some of these frequencies may be natural frequencies of the cranial, pleural or abdominal cavities of the human body; it is not inconceivable that, in the wrong infrasound environment, a person may burst like a wineglass, or at least haemorrhage internally. Sound can kill.

It can also be used in diagnosis. Currently the favoured method of examining foetuses *in utero* is not destructive X rays, but infrasound. High-pitched, unheard sound passes through the uterus to be absorbed or deflected by the foetus, thus building up a picture of what's going on inside. The use of sound in diagnosis is nothing new; the Pythagorean physicians developed a method which all doctors still use, called *auscultation*. The doctor taps the patient's chest or abdomen and listens to the way the sound passes through the pleural or abdominal cavity. Thus he builds up a mental picture of what's going on inside, identifying spots of congestion.

58

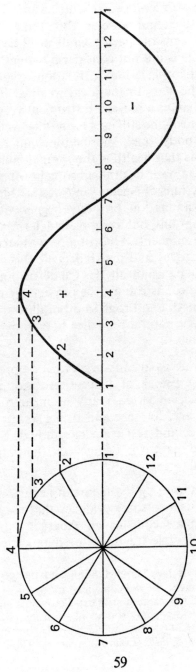

13. Basic wave form. This can represent virtually any type of rhythmic phenomenon: the shape of a vibrating string, pulsating energy, or – as shown here – the wave generated by a rotating wheel such as the zodiac or a planet's orbit.

Pythagoreans were concerned with natural life rhythms, such as the heartbeat and pulse and breathing. Irregularities in these are still signs of specific kinds of ill-health.

The Pythagoreans did not consider a patient in isolation, but tried instead to place him in relation to all outside influences, from the stars to the local weather. They carried the analogy of man as a musical instrument very far indeed, so that modern medicine still uses terms like 'well-tempered', 'temperament', 'body tone', 'muscle tone' and 'tonic'. Their essential idea was that health is the normal biological state, so that a person in poor health had somehow become out of tune with the rhythms of Nature, and was unable to respond properly. An examination properly began with not only the patient's symptoms, but a complete determination of the influences of the moment. A horoscope was erected for the time when the patient had first fallen ill; this was called a *decumbent*. With it, using all the Chaldean and Egyptian principles of medical astrology, the physician could attempt to predict the length and progress of an illness, and to find out which herbs or natural remedies to employ.

These physicians

believed when necessary in surgery. But more often they let the healing power of Nature proceed, unimpeded, while the physician stood ready to intrude only if absolutely necessary. Surgery and drugs were very seldom used, while diet and rest were paramount. Special diets were given, the main rule being *what* the patient wished to eat and could keep down.[4]

The treatments used by Pythagorean healers were mainly herbal, but there is also some evidence that they learned of vaccination from a Celtic healer, Abaris.* Far more important than any single treatment or diagnostic technique,

* Abaris was said to have founded the city of Bath (see p. 20 above). He is also said to have visited Pythagoras and shown him a 'sacred dart' by which he cured plagues and 'expelled winds and pestilences from the cities', which certainly sounds like vaccination. An account of this was written in 300 BC by Iamblichus; it is cited in John Ivimy, *The Sphinx and the Megaliths* (London: Abacus, 1976), pp. 96–7.

however, is the Pythagorean vision of harmony: The energy relationship between ourselves and the cosmos.

John M. Addey, president of the Astrological Association in Britain, has for some time been investigating longevity and disease and their relation to birth time. In one study he checked the birth charts of children in a polio hospital (where he teaches). The result was a graph showing a curious wave form he could not at first explain. He checked the

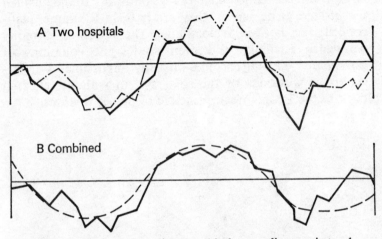

14. Pythagorean pattern in polio cases. (a) shows polio cases in two hospitals, (b) shows how they combine to produce the basic wave form.

births from a second hospital and found the same wave form, from the aspects of Mars to Mercury: 'Polio victims tended to be born according to the twelfth harmonic, and, most strongly of all, according to the 120th harmonic. Taken out of statistical language, Addey's chart means that a child born every third degree . . . is thirty-seven per cent more liable to contract polio than a child born in the two intermediary degrees.'[5] The wave form of the vibrating string is directly visible in the Addey graph (Figure 14). Once again we are reminded of harmonics: $\frac{1}{12}$ and $\frac{1}{120}$ belong to the basic series of Pythagoras. Indeed, all strong aspects belong to this same harmonic series:

Conjunction marks the complete circle, or the fundamental note of the series, 1.

Opposition (180°) marks the next note, $\frac{1}{2}$ (half the circle)
Trine (120°) marks the next note, $\frac{1}{3}$
Square (90°) marks the next note, $\frac{1}{4}$

The harmonic rhythm of planet movements is reflected not only in the aspects, but in the structure of the zodiac (as given in Chapter Two above):

If two planets are in conjunction, they are in the same sign. In square or opposition (negative aspects) they are both in the the same triplicity (eg, both in Fixed signs). In the positive trine aspect, they are both in the same quadruplicity (eg, both in Water signs). The notion of harmony permeates astrology and even guides the equations of *astronomy*.* Thus it becomes virtually impossible to understand the workings of the solar system without referring back to the Pythagorean principle of planet rhythms.

* To find out, for example, how often the Earth, Mars and the Sun will be in perfect alignment (a Mars–Sun conjunction), the space scientist uses the 'harmonic difference' of two values:

E = period of Earth's orbit around the Sun, 365¼ days
M = period of Mars' orbit around the Sun, 687 days
The harmonic difference gives the time between conjunctions, C:

$$\frac{1}{M} - \frac{1}{E} = \frac{1}{C}$$ giving C = 780 days approximately.

CHAPTER FIVE

The Wheel of Life

Signs, planets and aspects are not only important in themselves as indicators of health and disease, they are also important in the framework of the complete birth chart: the Twelve Houses.

The Houses are fixed divisions of the chart, relating the signs and planets to a particular time and place on Earth. As Figure 15 shows, the House divisions (called the *cusps* of the Houses) resemble a twelve-spoked wheel. The cusp of the First House is simply the Ascendant, giving the exact degree of the rising sign. The cusps of the other Houses are spaced equally, 30 degrees apart, around the circle.*

The top half of this wheel, Houses 7 to 12, represents that part of the sky which is visible above the horizon. The bottom half, Houses 1 to 6, represents that part which is hidden below the horizon. Whatever sign or planet is rising in the East is shown at the Ascendant, and whatever is setting in the West is shown at the 7th House cusp, or Descendant.

The twelve Houses and their attributes are:

1st House: The physical body and general health. As we saw in Chapter One, body type and general health are indicated by the Ascendant, which is the cusp of this House. The sign of the Ascendant gives the Native's 'background' of health, against which other factors in the chart will operate. Aries, for example, gives muscularity and energy. (The full delineation for each rising sign is given in Part Two of this book.) Any planet in this House has some influence on general health, and the closer the planet is to the Ascendant, the greater the influence. The 1st House shows most clearly

* Besides this 'equal-house' system, there is an older system of Houses called the Placidean, in which Houses are not of equal size.

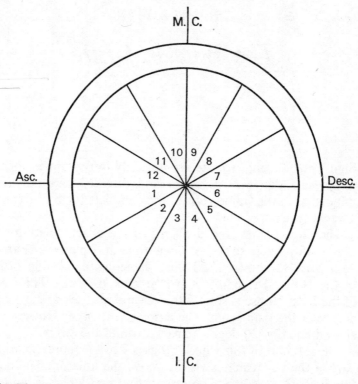

M. C.

Asc.

10 9 8
11 7
12
1 6
2 5
3 4

Desc.

I. C.

15. The Houses and angles. The Houses are numbered 1 to 12 counter-clockwise, beginning at the Ascendant. The four angles are the *Ascendant* (where we would find the Sun at dawn), the *Immum Coeli* or IC (where we would find it at midnight), the *Descendant* (at sunset) and the *Medium Coeli*, Midheaven or MC (at noon).

the health indications of *Aries* and its ruling planet, *Mars*.

2nd House: Money and possessions. This is also the House of the emotions, and any planet appearing here can give a clue to the Native's emotional outlook. Strongest health signs are those associated with *Taurus* and *Venus*. A hormone imbalance could be indicated by an ill-aspected planet here.

3rd House: Family ties, education, communication. This is the House of the mind and intellect, of speaking, writing and all forms of self-expression. Health indications resemble those of *Gemini* and *Mercury*.

4th House: Home life, parents, beginnings and endings. This is the chief house of inherited traits, including inherited susceptibility to disease. Health indications are those of *Cancer* and its ruling planet, the *Moon*.

5th House: Creativity, pleasure, children, games. An ill-aspected planet here can mean self-indulgence, which could lead to one of the diseases of indulgence, such as fatty degeneration of the heart. On the other hand, this House represents good health and vitality, especially in connection with the sign on the cusp or its ruling planet. Other health indications resemble those of *Leo* and the *Sun*.

6th House: Health and work. Any planet here refers to a tendency to disease of a specific type (as does the sign on the cusp, and the ruler of that sign). The tendency may be slight, but if the planet is ill-aspected by Saturn, Mars or Uranus, the Native should expect to be troubled, at some time in his life, by the indicated illness. For example, the Moon here could give a history of urinary infections or kidney stones. In general, the health indications of this House are those associated with *Virgo* and *Mercury*.

7th House: Partnerships, marriage, emotional relationships. The presence of any of the malefic planets (Saturn, Mars, Uranus, possibly Neptune and Pluto) at the *cusp* of this House could indicate diseases associated with *Libra* or its ruling planet, *Venus*). The House itself is not particularly indicative of illness, except for possible psychogenic complaints caused by a stressful emotional entanglement.

8th House: The life-force, birth and death, longevity. This House is a strong indicator of general health in later years. Capricorn on the cusp or Saturn well-placed within this House are said to indicate a long life. The Sun or Jupiter well-placed can mean good health in middle age and after. Other health and disease indications are those of *Scorpio* or *Mars*.

9th House: Travel, moral education, idealism. This House belongs to *Jupiter* and to the sign it rules, *Sagittarius*; Sagittarian complaints (eg, sciatica) can result from an ill-aspected planet here. However, it cannot be said that this House gives any strong warnings for health.

10th House: Aspirations, career, responsibilities. Any badly-placed planet here can mean a health problem resulting from overwork, fatigue or a stress condition brought on by the career. Generally the health indications are those for the planet *Saturn* and the sign *Capricorn*.

11th House: Friendship, social contacts, intellectual pastimes. The indications are those for *Uranus* and *Aquarius*. Uranus on the cusp can cause the Native to experience sudden, unexpected illnesses, but these seldom develop into long-term health problems.

12th House: Self-sacrifice, belief, seclusion. If several planets are in this House simultaneously it is said that the Native may suffer from 'negative escapism', leading to drink or drug problems. In general the indications are those applying to *Pisces* or *Neptune*.

Astrologers are particularly concerned with the effects of the four 'angles': the cusps of Houses 1, 4, 7 and 10. The cusp of the 1st House is of course the Ascendant; that of the 4th House is the nadir or lowest point (called the *Immum Coeli* and usually abbreviated 'IC'). The cusp of the 7th House is called the Descendant; that of the 10th House* is the Midheaven (called the *Medium Coeli* and abbreviated 'MC'). These four angles seem to be points of strong activity, and any planet at one of these angles is said to be particularly influential. The influence may be positive or negative, and this of course depends upon the planet and its aspects to the rest of the chart.

The most notable effects are those of the Ascendant and Midheaven. As we've seen, the Ascendant governs general health and outward physical appearance: the 'raw material' with which the Native begins his life. The Midheaven governs the career and the path through life – how the Native makes use of this raw material.

Since the 1950s, the Ascendant and Midheaven have turned up in science in an unexpected way – unexpected, that is, to non-astrologers. Michel Gauquelin of the Paraphysiological Laboratory at Strasbourg University began testing for the possible effects of planets on the careers of successful persons. Using *Who's Who* and similar directories,

---

* In some systems, the MC and the cusp of the 10th House are not considered to be the same point.

he took the names of 36,000 celebrities in many fields, checked their birth times, and examined planet positions for each birth.

He found that in any given field, an improbably large number of celebrities had the same planet rising (ie conjunct the Ascendant) or at its highest point (ie conjunct the Mid-heaven). Moreover, the critical planet for celebrities in any given profession was exactly the planet astrologers would expect to find: Mars, for example (traditionally associated with energy and physical aggression, and with the muscles) is the critical planet for champion athletes. For famous authors, the key planet is the Moon ('intuition, inspiration'). For famous actors, it is the expansive, 'extravert' planet Jupiter. For doctors and scientists, it is the cold, analytical planet Saturn.

A Belgian committee of astronomers, statisticians and demographers, unable to believe Gauquelin's results, re-peated his tests and confirmed them: Planets rising and at Midheaven really do seem to affect the lives of successful persons in many professions.[1]

Obviously not everyone born with Mars in a key position goes on to become a champion athlete. What Gauquelin's study means is that a person born with Mars Ascendant or Midheaven is more likely to possess or develop the kinds of qualities that are needed to be a champion athlete. If Mars is rising, we might expect him to possess such qualities from an early age; if at Midheaven, we might expect him to develop these qualities gradually.

What are these qualities and who has them? Gauquelin[2] gives summaries for the following planets:

MARS Ascendant or Midheaven strongly influences doctors, scientists, generals, sports champions, industrialists. *Key words*: active, eager, quarrelsome, reckless, combative, courageous, dynamic, energetic, fiery, untiring, fighting, aggressive, afraid of nothing, straightforward, strong, dar-ing, valiant, full of vitality, lively, self-willed.

JUPITER Ascendant or Midheaven strongly influences gen-erals, actors, politicians, journalists. *Key words*: at ease, ambitious, opportunistic, authoritarian, talkative, likes to assert himself, sense of the comical, communicative, debonair, spendthrift, bright, gesticulating often, good-humoured, independent, happy, worldly, prodigal, bantering, likeable, vain.

SATURN Ascendant or Midheaven strongly influences doctors, scientists. *Key words*: formal, reserved, conscientious, cold, methodical, modest, meticulous, observant, organized, not talkative, reflective, retiring, wise, melancholy, timid, industrious, silent, sad.

MOON Ascendant or Midheaven strongly influences writers (novelists and poets). *Key words*: amiable, many friends, simple, good company, good-hearted, accommodating, disorderly, absent-minded, generous, imaginative, easily influenced, fashionable, wordly, nonchalant, poetic, dreaming, obliging, rather snobbish, superficial, tolerant.

In medical terms, it is clear that character types like those above are part of the psychological make-up of the Natives concerned, and can therefore be the causes of psychogenic diseases. The Mars character is likely to be fit and active, not at all susceptible to illnesses that affect sedentary persons – but his recklessness can make him accident-prone. The ambitious Jupiter type could easily fall victim to stress complaints. The Saturnian may suffer from spells of depression or lassitude. The Lunar type may find his easy-going life-style leading to overweight and its attendant problems. A planet at one of the angles cannot, in any case, be safely ignored by the medical astrologer.

In these five chapters we have now seen all the basic principles of bioastrology:

The influence of the Rising sign
The influence of the Sun sign, Moon sign and planet signs
Zodiac structure and 'zodiac man'
The aspects between planets
The House influence
The four Angles

In Part Two, we can begin putting these into practice, reading the medical horoscope.

PART TWO

Signs of Life

Reading the Medical Horoscope

Setting up the natal horoscope is not an easy task. The beginner will find he needs an ephemeris (or table of planet positions), a table of Houses, and a good instructive guide (there are several excellent guides available[1]). Even then, the technical work can be daunting. But if you don't mind struggling through lengthy calculations of local sidereal time, you'll be rewarded with an extremely accurate birth chart. Early efforts should always be checked by a professional.

Another method is to use one of the many 'short cut' methods available,[2] to make a less accurate, but still useful chart. Or you may prefer to leave all the calculations to a professional – always a safe bet. In any case, you'll eventually come up with a chart such as that of Figure 16, ready for interpretation.

THE GENERAL METHOD

In any chart, the astrologer begins with the most general features and works down to particulars:

1. *The overall pattern of the planets*, whether they are distributed evenly or concentrated in certain signs and Houses. In Figure 16 Mr F is seen to have four of the ten planets in Pisces. The watery, emotional, compassionate nature of this sign is sure to be important in any assessment of Mr F. This is further confirmed by examining all the Water signs and negative signs: They contain seven planets each. Mr F begins to seem basically passive, unstressful, with much of the so-called feminine (unaggressive) in his character.

2. *The Sun sign*. Interpretations of all the Sun signs are given on pp. 79–142 below. Mr F has the Sun in 3° Pisces,

which should tend to make him idealistic, spiritual and dedicated to caring for others. He will probably be indecisive and impractical, and his concern for relieving the suffering of others could lead him to pursue a career in medicine or

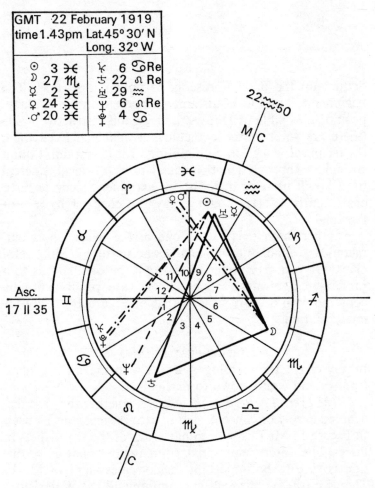

16. Horoscope at the birth of W.G.F. See text for analysis.

religion. Physically he will be susceptible to foot troubles and have a generally weak constitution, prey to passing colds and flu. But his constitution will be more clearly delineated by the sign of the Ascendant, as we'll see.

3. *The Moon sign.* Interpretations of the Moon signs are also on pp. 79–142 below. Mr F's Moon is in Scorpio, indicating more deep emotionality and perhaps a streak of pride or stubbornness. Possible diseases include bladder stones, hernia and some danger from poisons. Since Pisceans sometimes suffer from alcholism or drug dependence, we're entitled to wonder whether this doesn't refer to alcohol or drug poisoning. Could be, but the rest of the chart will tell.

4. *The Ascendant.* To find an Ascendant, you need the birth date and time – the more accurately, the better. Figure 17 gives a guide to the *sign* of the Ascendant (the Rising sign) for approximate times. Rising signs are interpreted on pp. 79–142 below.

Mr F has 17° 35′ Gemini rising. This could classify him as ectomorphic, tending to leanness, a slight build and neurasthenia. Neurasthenic persons often have a background of nervous exhaustion, job dissatisfaction, low spirits, and a general feeling of helplessness in the face of their problems. Geminians often have weak chests.

Pisces and Gemini are both 'dual' signs, indicating a measure of indecisiveness, and this could be a serious problem for Mr F. In any case, he probably has a weak constitution, as his Sun sign hinted.

5. *The planets*, their signs, Houses and aspects. The Sun and Moon signs have already been discussed for Mr F. Their Houses, along with the Houses and signs for other planets, are covered on pp. 79–164 below. The Sun is in the 9th House there, showing more of Mr F's tendency to colds and flu. Since the Moon is in the 6th House, the House of specific diseases, we have a much stronger indication of danger from poisons. Moreover, bladder stones or kidney stones are a distinct possibility.

Mercury is in Pisces in the 9th House: Possible memory defects arising from mental exhaustion.

Venus is in Pisces in the 10th House: Possible bronchial colds accompanied by headaches (especially in a weak-chested Native).

The positions of Mars (Pisces, 10th House) and Saturn

73

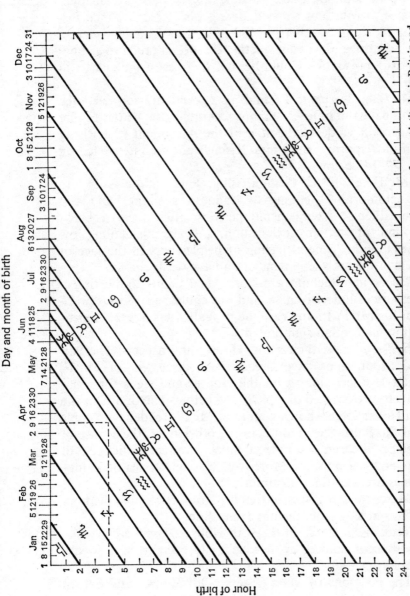

Day and month of birth

Hour of birth

17. Ascendant chart. This gives ascendants for most latitudes in Britain and Europe. To use the chart, find the date closest to your month and day of birth at the top, find your hour of birth at the left, and use a straightedge or the edge of a card to locate the correct zone as shown. In the example, someone born at 4 a.m. on 9 April has *Aquarius* rising.

74

(Leo, 3rd House) both indicate possible chest pains or inflammation.

Jupiter (Cancer, 1st House) indicates that, despite his general weakness, Mr F may have some resistance to disease. He may in fact be healthier than we've so far thought, though much will depend on the aspects.

Uranus (29° of Aquarius, 9th House) could indicate sudden cramps in legs or feet.

Neptune (Leo, 2nd House) gives another drug warning.

In order to test these planetary indications, we must examine the aspects. Two planets are said to be in aspect not only when they are at an *exact* angular distance apart, but when they are close to this distance: a few degrees allowance, or *orb* can be made:

	Aspect		Orb		Aspect		Orb
☌	Conjunction	(0°)	8°	⌑	Sesquiquadrate	(135°)	2°
☍	Opposition	(180°)	8°	✳	Sextile	(60°)	6°
☐	Square	(90°)	8°	⊼	Quincunx	(150°)	3°
△	Trine	(120°)	8°	∟	Semi-square	(45°)	2°
				⊻	Semi-sextile	(30°)	2°

In the case of Mr F, the Sun (3° Pisces) and Mercury (2° Pisces) are in conjunction because they are less than 8° apart.

The easiest way to keep track of all the aspects is to make an 'aspect grid' as shown in Figure 18.

The strongest patterns have already been marked on Mr F's chart (Figure 16). *Negative aspects*: Mercury and Sun are in conjunction, opposed to Saturn and square the Moon. This pattern, shown by the heavy black triangle on the chart, indicates a tendency to one of the diseases of hysteria. The Sun conjunct Uranus emphasizes this tendency. Taking into account what we've seen in the overall pattern, it is possible to guess which disease is indicated: Neurasthenia, or emotional and nervous exhaustion.

Positive aspects: Venus conjunct Mars trine the Moon. The trine is always a positive, restorative force in the chart, and here it is the lunar influence which acts to restore the balance of a personality threatened by almost schizophrenic

75

division. Venus and Mars (in the dual sign of Pisces) pull Mr F's personality in two directions, but their splitting action is softened by the Moon's soothing influence.

Jupiter trine the Sun–Mercury conjunction is also positive. In ancient times Jupiter was associated with wealth, but now this is taken to mean freedom from material concerns and cares. That the Sun and Mercury are in Pisces shows that this freedom arises from a strong spirituality. In

	Sign	House	☽	☿	♀	♂	♃	♄	♅	♆	♇	A	MC	
☉	3 ♓	9	□	☌	·	·	△	·	☍	⊼	·	·	·	☉
☽	27 ♍	6		·	△	△	·	□	□	·	·	·	□	☽
☿	2 ♓	9			·	·	△	·	☌	⊼	·	·	·	☿
♀	24 ♓	10				☌	·	⊼	·	·	·	□	⊻	♀
♂	20 ♓	10					·	⊼	·	·	·	□	⊻	♂
♃	6 ♋ Re	1						∟	·	⊻	☌	·	⊡	♃
♄	22 ♌ Re	2							·	·	·	·	☍	♄
♅	29 ♒	9								·	·	·	☍	♅
♆	6 ♌ Re	2									⊻	∟	؛	♆
♇	4 ♋	1										·	·	♇
A	17 ♊ 35	–											·	A
MC	22 ♒ 50	–												MC

18. Aspect grid for W.G.F. (See birth chart, Figure 16).

physical terms it means that Mr F is remarkably free of stress and likely to weather any sudden or serious bouts of illness produced by the negative aspects.

6. *The four Angles.* The next step is to look to the 1st, 4th, 7th and 10th Houses: ill-aspected planets here could mean specific illnesses.

In Mr F's 1st House are Jupiter and Pluto in conjunction. Jupiter's positive influence is much stronger than any putative negative influence of Pluto, and the Jupiter–Sun trine also indicates basic good health. At least we can say that Mr F's constitution in childhood was resistant to disease, despite a weak chest.

The 4th House has no planets, so we look to the sign on

76

the cusp, Virgo. The ruler of this sign is Mercury, planet of the nerves and lungs. As we've seen already, Mr F is somewhat prone to nervousness and a weak chest.

The 7th House has no planets, so we look to the sign on the cusp, Sagittarius. Its ruler is Jupiter, which is well-placed: No problems.

The 10th House brings us once again to the duality of Pisces and the Venus–Mars conjunction. As we've seen, the Moon modifies this unpleasant indication of emotional tension.

7. *Specific diseases in the 6th House*: Here we find the Moon in 27 degrees of Scorpio, afflicted by Saturn, portending urinary infections, kidney or bladder stones, hernia, venereal disease – something connected with the urinary tract. Venereal disease is less likely because of the Moon's trine to Venus, but the other ailments are distinct possibilities. Lunar Scorpions are also in some danger from poisons, including food poisoning.

8. *The 8th House and longevity.* Length of life can often be estimated by comparing the Sun sign to the influence of the 8th House. Here the Sun is in Pisces, traditionally a short-lived sign, while the sign on the 8th House cusp is Capricorn, sign of long life. There is, then, an apparent contradiction.

In practice such apparent contradictions can only be settled by the health astrologer's experience and judgement, taking into consideration the rest of the chart. In this case there are no serious physical ailments which could account for Mr F's having a short life, with the possible exception of poisoning. If his Piscean nature asserts itself, Mr F could well develop drink or drug habits, or possibly a smoking habit, which would shorten his life (probably by damage to heart, lungs or kidneys). If, however, he is fairly abstemious in his habits, Mr F could live to a ripe old Capricornian age. It's up to him.

9. *Prevention and remedy.* The final stage in interpreting the birth chart is determining how the Native can best combat his designated illnesses. If the illness has not yet appeared, he or she can prevent it in many cases by proper diet

and by developing positive habits to counteract the negative indications of his chart. For each Sun sign, suggested dietary requirements and habits are listed on pp. 79–142.

The Native who is ill should of course see his or her doctor. If the doctor is, as some modern practitioners are, trained also in astrological diagnosis, so much the better. Some complaints respond to herbal remedies associated with the appropriate signs or planets. A list of herbs and their use is given under each Sun sign on pp. 79–142.

10. *Alternatives and refinements.* When a chart turns out to be particularly puzzling or ambiguous, the health astrologer may wish to clarify it by reference to other systems, such as those given in Part Four of this book.

CHAPTER ONE

Aries ♈

Sun sign period: 21 March to 19 April
Ruling planet: Mars ♂
  Mars makes those it governs decisive, freedom-loving,
  pioneering, courageous, strongly sexed, energetic, aggres-
  sive, impatient, angry and liable to accidents and injuries
Polarity: Positive or masculine (extraverted, active, stressful,
  'type A' persons)
Element: Fire (enthusiasm, haste)
Nature: Cardinal (enterprising, outgoing)

ARIES, THE RAM is symbolised by a pair of curled ram's horns.
No doubt the ancient shepherds of Babylon watched the
head-on clashes of rams during the first warm month of
spring, and so took the Ram as the embodiment of all that
is combative and headstrong in human nature. Aries rules
the head, upper brain functions, eyes and upper jaw. By
reflex to Libra, it reacts upon the kidneys.

SUN SIGN: Ariens tend to be direct, enthusiastic 'go-getters',
willing to try anything and often impatient to forge ahead.
If you are born with the Sun in this active, pioneering sign,
you are likely to be ambitious, aggressive and ready to take
risks to reach your goal. You have little trouble in deciding
what you want and going after it in the most direct manner,
though often without thinking of the consequences. You
may take a difficult or dangerous job, for you get real
pleasure from meeting obstacles head-on and knocking
them aside. Of course this tendency has its drawbacks:
Ariens are seldom tactful or diplomatic, and are often found
trampling heedlessly on the feelings of others. They can also

be quick-tempered – especially in dealing with over-cautious people – or wilful and selfish.

The Arien is the originator of grand schemes, which usually involve plenty of hard work and initiative. But he tends to overlook details and become impatient when others fail to see his point of view. You are unlikely to be really happy working for anyone who lacks your drive, vision and courage, or in any stale, everyday job with no immediate prospects for advancement. You have little time for patiently climbing the ladder of success, whether in your profession or social relationships – you probably prefer short cuts, quick answers and immediate gratification.

You may act as though your physical and mental energy were boundless, but of course it is not. There is a real danger of overwork, of physical and mental exhaustion, and of abusing your system through lack of care. Ariens usually have general good health and strong constitutions – but both can be destroyed through (typically Arien) stress and strife. Learn to take it easy, to let things slide a bit. Try not to meet every foe and every problem head-on.

Symptoms and diseases: Ariens tend to suffer from tension headaches, migraine, eyestrain, tiredness, loss of weight, stress-connected diseases, stroke, meningitis (inflammation of membranes of the brain), head colds, fevers, impaired memory, dizzy spells, skin eruptions. (See also *Note* at the end of this chapter.)

Diet: Your diet should include foods containing your bio-chemic salt, potassium phosphate: tomatoes, beets, celery, lettuce, cauliflower, watercress, spinach, onions, mustard greens, radishes, carrots, cucumbers, dates, apples, walnuts and lemons. Your diet *must* include foods rich in iron and protein, to help rebuild the blood and muscle destroyed by your habits of overwork. These foods include lean meats, milk, cheese, eggs, beans, peas and other legumes, soya meat-substitutes and real bread.

It would be wise to avoid foods containing highly saturated fats in large quantities, which many doctors believe contribute to hardening of the arteries. Avoid nicotine entirely, and keep your intake of caffeine (coffee, tea or cola drinks) to a minimum. Use alcohol very moderately, not only because it can make you more combative than ever, but because, like caffeine or nicotine, it could make a stroke more likely. Strokes are caused by high blood pressure bursting hardened blood vessels in the brain.

The most important factor in Arien diet is not food at all, but how and when it is eaten. Ariens all too often grab a quick meal without noticing what they're stuffing down, or eat during times of stress when digestion is difficult. You should try to develop the habit of eating slowly and thoughtfully, and only when your body (rather than a clock on the wall) signals that it's mealtime.

Herbs: Cayenne pepper (*Capsicum frutiscens*), ruled by Mars. This is said by Culpeper* to relieve toothache: boil the husks of the pepper and rinse the mouth with this decoction.

Blackberry (*Rubus fruticosus*), ruled by Venus in Aries. Culpeper recommends it for a variety of Arien complaints: The leaves may be boiled to make a shampoo that relieves itching of the scalp; a lotion made from pressing the leaves and buds is said to heal gumboils; the fruit makes a soothing syrup for sore throats (not only delicious, but full of Vitamin C).

Sweet marjoram (*Origanum marjorana*), ruled by Mercury in Aries. According to Leon Petulengro, the fresh herb infused in boiling water is a good headache cure.

Holy thistle (*Carduus benedictus*), ruled by Mars in Aries. Culpeper claims that a cordial of this reduces fever.

Peppermint (*Mentha piperita*), ruled by Mars. Good for settling the stomach.

Garlic (*Allium sativum*), ruled by Mars. This herb has

* Sources for all herbal information in this part: Nicholas Culpeper, *Culpeper's Complete Herbal* (London: W. Foulsham & Co. Ltd, n.d.); D. and J. Parker, *The Compleat Astrologer* (London: Mitchell Beazley, 1975); Omar V. Garrison, *Medical Astrology* (New York: Warner Paperback Library, 1973); Dr J. A. S. Sage, *Live To Be a Hundred* (London: Star Books, 1975); Leon Petulengro, 'Astrological guide to herbs and healing' in *Woman's Own*, 22 and 29 January 1977.

almost too many virtues to list here. People have chewed it to clear the sinuses and to give relief in asthma (chewing cumin seeds afterwards can help sweeten the breath); it can be used for mouth ulcers or sore throat likewise; Culpeper recommends it for 'wind colic'; it is now known to have germ-killing properties; Petulengro claims it relieves 'ills of the gastric tract'.

Horseradish (*Cochlearia armoracia*), ruled by Mars. Eating horseradish is good for skin troubles, asthma and rheumatic pains, according to Dr J. A. S. Sage. Culpeper claims that the bruised root, laid upon aching joints, eases them.

Emotional life: The Arien has a strong sexual drive that must be expressed. All too often, it is expressed selfishly. The Arien is an ardent and capable lover, but can be rather childish when emotional problems arise.

Profession: Anything fast, dangerous or exciting which doesn't involve taking too many orders. Ariens often go into sports, and most often fast, competitive, solo sports: racing cars or motorcycles, boxing, wrestling, tennis, soccer, basketball or hockey. Ariens can be explorers, research workers, firemen and professional soldiers.

Biorhythm risk days: (explanation on p. 198).

P	E	I
+	c	c
−	c	c
−	+	c
+	−	c
c	+	−

Habits: Avoid losing your temper over trifles, the need to have your own way, obstinacy, heavy workloads, hard drinking and smoking, impatience. Try to develop tolerance, a bit of laziness, and the ability to lose an argument gracefully.

MOON SIGN: Born with the Moon in Aries, you are likely to be quick-witted but also quick to anger. Lunar Ariens are often sincere, likeable people and natural leaders, but they can also be headstrong and impatient, unwilling to accept orders or advice. At the same time, they may be indecisive. This may in fact be the secret of their charm: There's something warmly human about a leader who sometimes gets lost. Especially if, like the typical lunar Arien, he has a sense of humour.

Physically, you may be susceptible to fevers, insomnia, headaches, weak eyes and dandruff or falling hair. Nothing serious here, but you also may suffer from a slight degree of accident-proneness (see *Note* below).

RISING SIGN: Those born with Aries Rising have clearcut features, high foreheads and cheekbones, decisive chins and a general look of firmness. The brows are likely to be heavy, the nose longer than average, and there may be a widow's peak. The body type is *mesomorphic*, tending to muscularity.

The Ascendant Arien is strongly sexed, but deeply romantic. If born at sunrise, he may have trouble reconciling these two conflicting sides of his nature.

Note: Solar Ariens whose Sun is afflicted, and all lunar Ariens, show a tendency to accident-proneness. The Martial rulership of this sign encourages foolhardy and reckless behaviour, such as fast and careless driving. Accidents involving fire or sharp instruments are also indicated.

CHAPTER TWO

Taurus ♉

Sun sign period: 20 April to 20 May
Ruling planet: Venus ♀
    Venus encourages love, attraction, partnerships, the feminine character in both sexes; love of beauty, harmony, money and possessions, gentleness, a placid nature, artistic sensibilities, fine feelings
Polarity: Negative or feminine (introverted, passive, 'type B' persons)
Element: Earth (practical, methodical)
Nature: Fixed (enduring)

TAURUS, THE BULL is symbolized by a horned bull's head. In ancient Greece, the bull represented beauty and fertility: According to the legend, Zeus disguised himself as a white bull with golden horns, seduced the maiden Europa into climbing upon his neck, and carried her away into the sea. The bull's neck is its strength, as matadors know; they weaken the neck muscles before the kill. Taurus rules the throat, neck, Eustachian tubes, carotid artery, larynx, tonsils, neck vertebrae of the spine, thyroid gland and lower brain functions. By reflex to Scorpio, Taurus reacts upon the sex organs.

SUN SIGN: The Taurean is a quiet, reliable, home-loving person, with a down-to-earth, practical nature that encourages others to rely upon him. Born in this earthy, steady sign, you probably prefer a quiet life, pleasant home surroundings, good food and luxuries. Your ruling planet Venus gives you a deep appreciation of art or music, beauty in your environment and sensual pleasures. Commonly

Taureans are patrons of the arts, or artists.

You have a patient, methodical way of working through your problems slowly, and with a persistence that pays off. You may well be good at business, unless rapid decisions are called for – speed is seldom a Taurean trait. Your home life should be tranquil and pleasurable, partly because your patient nature helps iron out difficulties without resorting to bickering. Of course Taureans do lose their tempers, but seldom over small things, and usually only when their great reserves of patience have been exhausted. You probably dislike travelling, are glad to get home again, and in general prefer familiar pastures to greener grass elsewhere. For the same reason, you are a faithful lover and a reliable friend as well as a willing worker – *but*:

Taureans can, at worst, be lazy, unexciting and unoriginal thinkers. They tend to get tied to humdrum jobs or home routines, and they may care too much about their possessions. At best, they are thoughtful, warm people, comfortable to be with, and certainly the most easy-going of friends.

As a Taurean you tend to overeat and to avoid exercise, so you are inclined to put on weight easily. If over forty, this means that you are in real danger: Your weight should not exceed twenty per cent of the average for your height and age, or you run the risk of serious heart and circulatory diseases.

Symptoms and diseases: Taureans commonly suffer from throat infections, goitre, asthma, sinus infections, neuralgia in neck muscles, ear infections and dental problems (usually of the lower jaw). But they also tend to worry too much about their health, and should guard against becoming hypochondriacs. Taurean resistance to infection is normally good, unless afflicted planets in the chart indicate otherwise.

Diet: The most important part of Taurean diet is holding down your weight. It's essential to start restricting your intake of carbohydrates as soon as you notice your weight rising, and to begin a sensible regimen of exercise. Better still, try to develop the habit of sensible diet and exercise at all times. Many Taureans are fond of gardening, and this can be an excellent way to take enough exercise almost without noticing it; so are walking, light calisthenics or Yoga. In any case, try to cut down on sweets, sugar and those high-calorie desserts Taureans seem to crave.

Your biochemic salt is sodium sulphate, which helps prevent water retention in the body. It can be found in fresh spinach, cauliflower (especially in the green parts), beets, radishes, onions, cabbage and pumpkin.

You may have a dietary deficiency of iodine, the input for the thyroid gland. Those suffering from iodine deficiency are likely to develop goitre. Common iodine sources are seafood, sea salt, iodized salt, and root vegetables such as carrots and beets.

Herbs: Sage (*Salvia officinalis*), ruled by Jupiter in Taurus. The juice of fresh sage taken in warm water helps hoarseness and coughing (Culpeper). Adding sage makes a bath refreshing in summer.

Yarrow (*Achillea ptarmica*), ruled by Venus. This is called sneeze-wort, because the powdered leaves snuffed up the nose were used to clear the head, especially the sinuses.

Colt's foot (*Tussilago farfara*), ruled by Venus. 'The fresh leaves, or juice, or syrup thereof, is good for a hot, dry cough,' says Culpeper.

Figwort (*Scrophularia nodosa*), ruled by Venus in Taurus. The bruised root of this, applied to bruises, is thought to reduce the swelling.

Thyme (*Thymus vulgaris*), ruled by Venus. Strengthens the lungs, and in an ointment 'takes away hot swellings' (Culpeper). Good for settling the stomach, taken as thyme tea.

Lovage (*Ligusticum levisticum*), ruled by the Sun in Taurus. From medieval times the root of lovage was used to clear the skin. The root is boiled and the water then boiled down to strengthen it; washing the face with this liquid is then said to clear blemishes.

Emotional life: Taureans are sensual, passive, affectionate lovers, with a great deal of charm. They are faithful, and expect fidelity in return. They are in danger of becoming too settled in their ways, too satisfied with an unexciting, routine domestic life and of being too possessive.

Profession: Taureans like routine and security, so are often attracted into solid professions like banking, business, finance, accounting, and the civil service. Their love of beauty may combine with their natural acquisitiveness to make them art dealers, or they may try tedious but artistic work like jewellery-making, watch-making, stone sculpture or architecture. Other Taureans (everything depends upon the rest of the birth chart) prefer gardening, horticulture or farming – anything to do with the soil. It should be no surprise that many Taureans become singers, for Venus rules music and the Bull's domain is the throat. In medieval zodiacs, the Bull's horns were shown as a lyre.

Biorhythm risk days: (explanation on p. 198).

P	E	I
c	+	c
c	c	−
c	−	+
+	−	−
c	+	−

Habits: You should avoid laziness, getting into a rut, jealousy, possessiveness, overeating. Try to develop a fresh outlook, new ideas, optimism and a sense of humour.

MOON SIGN: Those born with the Moon in Taurus are likely to be good at handling or making money, sociable, sensual and friendly. Unlike solar Taureans they probably have a well-developed sense of humour and an optimistic outlook, but they are equally possessive and domesticated. They are likely to have some musical talent.

Lunar diseases include quinsy, sore throats, laryngitis, mouth ulcers, tonsillitis and eye infections. Also (by reflex from Scorpio), women born with the Moon in Taurus are subject to irregular menstruation or period pains.

RISING SIGN: Those born with Taurus Rising commonly have round foreheads, protruding eyes, a fleshy jaw and a thick neck. The thick neck is most noticeable in those born with 15° to 29° Taurus Rising. A firm mouth and a pleasant smile is usual.

The body type of Ascendant Taureans is *endomorphic*, tending to muscle or fat, with a generally heavy build.

CHAPTER THREE

Gemini ♊

Sun sign period: 21 May to 21 June
Ruling planet: Mercury ☿
  Mercury promotes cleverness, quick wits, intellect and
  versatility. Those born under its influence are good with
  languages, logical in debate; nervous, quick-moving,
  flighty, glib and aimless
Polarity: Positive or masculine (extraverted, active, stressful
  'type A' persons)
Element: Air (intellectual and communicative)
Nature: Mutable (changing, adaptable)

GEMINI, THE TWINS are symbolized by two pillars. This sign
was called the Great Twins in Babylon; Castor and Pollux,
the mythic twins in Greece; and in India, The Lovers. It
represents a basic duality in human nature, and of course
corresponds to the basic symmetry of the human body.
Gemini rules the nerves, arms, shoulders, the lungs and
respiration, and (by reflex) the liver.

SUN SIGN: The Geminian is the communicator of the zodiac.
Speech and writing are what he does best – and most often.
Born with the Sun in this versatile, intellectual sign, you
probably have a talent for thinking, writing or speaking
clearly, a lively and talkative nature, and a keen wit. You
can take almost any side in any argument and win – or at
least convince your opponent that he's lost, somehow. In
arguments the Geminian is quick, constantly changing his
mind, and seeming to have no fixed opinions of his own.
Usually he's a skilled debater and knows a little about a lot
of subjects, and he knows how to bluff – all attributes of an

89

agile mind that seldom allows him to be cornered. Needless to say, Geminians often make good lawyers or barristers, successful sales persons and keen journalists.

The Geminian can also give the appearance of being nosey, a gossip and hypocritical. He is fickle in personal relationships, often unreliable in any job that requires persistence. The Geminian likes to begin projects and usually has half-a-dozen going at once, leaping from one to another. But, though he works hard at all of them, he seldom seems to finish what he starts.

You thrive on variety, and a frequent change of job or scene. You like travelling, trying new flirtations or new social relationships, encountering new ideas. Your dual nature makes you capable of seeing more than one viewpoint at the same time.

Physically your duality may mean that you are ambidexterous. It is likely that you look younger than your real age, and you are lively, energetic and nervous. Since Geminians tend to 'live on their nerves', nervous exhaustion is always a danger.

Symptoms and diseases: Geminians are alert, active, twenty-five-hour-a-day people who plunge into a dozen activities at once. Despite your generally youthful, sturdy constitution, overwork and exhaustion can bring on a number of ailments besides nervous collapse. You are especially prone to diseases of the lungs and arms: Bronchitis, chest colds, emphysema, neuralgia of the shoulders and arms, 'tennis elbow', pneumonia.

Diet: You may be deficient in calcium or vitamin D (which is necessary to enable the body to absorb calcium). Milk contains both in good quantities. Calcium is also to be found in cheese, eggs, yoghurt, spinach, watercress, parsley, turnip greens and kale. If a vitamin D supplement is required, cod liver oil is the richest supply, containing up to 5800 times as much as milk.

Proteins are important to the energetic Geminian: get them from lean meats, fish, eggs, milk products and legumes. You may be underweight, but unless this makes you feel run-down, it is not necessarily a problem. Being slightly underweight is in fact a good way of maintaining your Geminian youthful looks and energy.

The Gemini cell salt, potassium chloride, is best obtained from asparagus, beets, carrots, cauliflower, celery, sweet corn, green beans, peaches, plums, pineapple and cherries.

All too often, Geminians 'dine' on a cigarette and a cup of strong coffee or tea. The smoking danger to *your* lungs should be obvious, and caffeine, for the nervy Geminian type, probably contributes to insomnia.

Herbs: Licorice (*Glycyrrhiza glabra*), ruled by Mercury. In a syrup, for coughs.

Parsley (*Carum petroselinum*), ruled by Mercury. Eating parsley not only provides vitamins and minerals, it helps stop flatulence, vomiting and wind, and tones up the alimentary system (Petulengro).

Lavender (*Lavendula vera*), ruled by Mercury. Formerly people cured nervousness by sucking lumps of sugar sprinkled with lavender water. For dizziness Culpeper recommends a decoction made of lavender flowers, horehound, fennel, asparagus and a pinch of cinnamon; also for laryngitis, two spoonfuls of lavender water.

Dill (*Antheum graveolens*), ruled by Mercury. Boiled in water or white wine, it is good for stopping vomiting, also as a hiccough cure.

Red clover (*Trifolium pratens*), ruled by Mercury. Culpeper suggests making it into a poultice for soothing inflammation.

Vervain (*Verbena officinalis*), ruled by Venus in Gemini. An old remedy for coughs and strengthener of the stomach; Culpeper claims that, mixed with honey, it helps heal wounds.

Emotional life: Geminians are not over-emotional. In love they can express themselves well in writing or talking, and they frequently flirt. The dual nature of this sign makes it possible for its natives to see both sides of emotional questions, so they are seldom deeply involved. They may have two mistresses or lovers, or have an extra-marital affair despite a reasonably satisfactory home life.

Profession: Anything to do with talking, writing, travelling or communications: journalist, radio or TV worker, author, travelling salesman, postman, travel agent, pilot, driver, electronics engineer (especially in communications), barrister, actor, telephone operator, translator or interpreter.

Biorhythm risk days: (explanation on p. 198)

P	E	I
+	c	c
c	—	c
+	c	—
c	—	—
c	+	—

Habits: The first three things to avoid are smoking, smoking and smoking. Stop kidding yourself that, because you've never had health problems in the past, smoking can't harm you. (This is typically Geminian 'double-think'.) While smoking is dangerous for anyone, you are especially vulnerable. It's probably just as well to avoid alcohol and stimulants; your naturally frenetic nature doesn't need stimulation, and they could lead to insomnia.

Try to develop your lungs by regular, light outdoor exercise, such as walking, running, bicycling. Develop the habit of taking yourself, and your health, more seriously. Emotionally you'll be more at ease if you develop the habit of speaking with forethought and sincerity. Mean what you say, and make promises only if you can keep them.

MOON SIGN: Those born with the Moon in Gemini can be extremely restless, troubled by insomnia, nervous tension and spells of overexcitement. Often they are highly intelligent, and their quick, creative minds can shuffle facts adroitly. At the same time, they may have trouble telling the truth; if the Moon is badly afflicted, they may even practise fraud.

Diseases linked with the Moon in Gemini include bronchitis, asthma, insomnia, pleurisy and rheumatic chest pains.

RISING SIGN: Gemini Rising gives its natives oval faces with small chins, and regular features. Brows are arched, nose thin and slightly aquiline, mouth mobile and indecisive. The body type is *ectomorphic*, tending to leanness and a slight build.

CHAPTER FOUR

Cancer ♋

Sun sign period: 22 June to 21 July
Ruling planet: The Moon ☽
 The Moon governs instinct, intuition, the emotions;
 patience, passiveness, imagination. Those born under its
 influence are shrewd, receptive, sensitive and sympathetic,
 have a retentive memory and sudden changes of mood
Polarity: Negative or feminine (introverted, passive, 'type B'
 persons)
Element: Water (emotional, intuitive, unstable)
Nature: Cardinal (enterprising)

CANCER, THE CRAB is symbolized by a pair of claws. In
Babylon it was *Allul*, a water-creature; in Egypt, two turtles,
and in early Greece, the Tortoise. In all cultures it was
associated with a hard-shelled water-creature for two reasons: It is a lunar, watery sign, unpredictable as a sudden
tide, or a sudden mood. It also represents the softness inside
the hard shell. Cancer rules the stomach and alimentary
canal.

SUN SIGN: It's ironic that the Cancerian is so often a kind,
sympathetic, understanding person, because other people
seldom understand or sympathize with the Cancerian. The
problem is moodiness. At times the Cancerian is thoughtful
and sensitive, ready to listen to the problems of others. But
without warning, his mood can change. His sensitivity turns
inward, he becomes touchy and easily slighted and ready to
take offence at nothing.
 Born with the Sun in this sensitive, imaginative sign, you
tend to take life very seriously; those who can match your

changing moods will find you a valuable friend and a loving companion. You are or could be a protective, understanding parent and an excellent homemaker. In business, the Cancerian usually shows a cool shrewdness, a rare knack for financial success, yet a sensible degree of caution. When it comes to understanding the hidden feelings of others, you sometimes seem almost psychic, capable of achieving a rapport that is rare. Those who know you less well may think of you as hard-headed, but this is just the shell; inside, the Crab is soft and vulnerable.

You are probably fond of collecting things. This can lead to an occupation (such as banking or antique dealing), a minor mania (saving string and paper bags) or it can simply turn to family feeling: You probably enjoy a gathering of the clan, especially at a lavish meal.

Cancerians love to cook and eat, so over-indulgence is their weakness. Probably for this reason, they are often troubled with both weight problems and digestive disorders.

Symptoms and diseases: Cancerian stomachs can't take the strain expected of them. Commonest complaints are indigestion, heartburn, gastric ulcers, hiccoughs, flatulence, diarrhoea, hyper-acidity and gallstones.

Diet: You are likely to have erratic eating habits. At times you pile on the food and drink, even to excess. At other times you try 'crash diets' and fasting, or follow the latest popular health diet. Real health does not come from such stop-go eating habits, or from any one 'miracle' health food. Remember that all natural foods are good for you, taken in moderation and in a balanced diet. Try to avoid stuffing yourself when you feel depressed or annoyed – as you possibly do all too often. Instead, keep mealtime atmospheres as calm and friendly as possible, for the sake of your stomach.

If, like many Cancerians, you tend to put on weight, crash diets are no answer. The best diet for you is simply to eat what your *body* feels it needs, when it needs it – but don't eat quite as much as your *psyche* calls for.

Cancerians are by nature worriers, so ulcers are certainly

a possibility. The best cure here is prevention: Begin by learning to trust people, especially those closest to you, and to forgive and forget injuries. Develop the ability to switch off your worries, whether by meditation, prayer, Yoga breathing exercises or any other means (such as biofeedback therapy). Take smaller meals, more often, and include milk in each.

Your cell salt is calcium fluoride, found in skim milk, cheese, kale, watercress, cabbage, eggs and dried fruits. Protein may be lacking in your diet, as a result of your filling up on sugars and starches. Try more lean meats, especially chicken, eggs, cottage cheese, skim milk and crispbread. If you really 'need' sugar, get it from honey. Honey has only three-quarters of the calorific content of white sugar, and it also contains several vital trace elements. A spoonful of it a day, with live yoghurt, can do no harm to any diet.

Herbs: Balm (*Melissa officinalis*), ruled by Jupiter in Cancer. Useful, as its name implies, in skin lotions. Its lemon scent is a delight.

Saxifrage (*Saxifraga alba*), ruled by the Moon. Good for diarrhoea, colic, upset stomachs. The young shoots are delicious in a salad.

Clary (*Salvia*), ruled by the Moon. Clary leaves boiled can make a 'tea' that aids digestion.

Black Alder (*Alnus nigra*), ruled by Venus in Cancer. Culpeper calls it a purgative, but it is best to consult his *Herbal* directly before experimenting with it; it is potent, and if misused, downright poisonous.

Daisy (*Chrysanthemum leucanthemum*), ruled by Venus in Cancer. Culpeper describes the juice of daisies or boiled daisies as used in oils, ointments, plasters and syrup. Handy for healing wounds, reducing swelling and soothing bruises, this herb is also useful for heartburn.

Duckweed (*Lens palustris*), ruled by the Moon in Cancer. Can be used in a poultice with barley meal to soothe inflammation. The leaves applied to the forehead can relieve headache.

Agrimony (*Agrimonia eupatoria*), ruled by Jupiter in Cancer. A decoction in wine is cleansing and good for cough or stomach ache. The leaves have long been used directly for healing small wounds and drawing splinters.

Betony (*Betonica aquatica*), ruled by Jupiter in Cancer. Mixed with honey, the bruised leaves make a good lotion for skin blemishes or small cuts and scrapes.

Honeysuckle (*Lonicorna caprifolium*), ruled by Mars in Cancer. The oil taken from the leaves by infusion is warm and soothing, and may be applied to relieve muscular cramps.

Emotional life: Complicated. Cancerians are timid and moody, but have a sensual imagination, indicative of a healthy sex life. As husbands they may be over-protective; as wives, snappish and irritable; but it seldom prevents them from building sound homes and family lives. Cancerians are loving parents.

Profession: Thrift, parental feeling, and an enjoyment of feeding others can lead Cancerians to such professions as banking, business, nursing, cooking, teaching or dealing with small children. Museum curator, antique dealer, historian are also likely professions, since Cancerians have excellent memories and like gathering up collections. They fare well as market gardeners, dieticians, or fishermen.

Biorhythm risk days: (explanation on p. 198)

P	E	I
c	+	c
—	+	—
—	+	c
—	—	+
c	c	+

Habits: Avoid worry, self-pity, bearing grudges, overeating. Try to develop cheerfulness, optimism, more confidence in yourself and in those you love.

MOON SIGN: The familial, paternal or maternal feeling is highly developed in lunar Cancerians. They have a strong

imagination and a deep reservoir of sympathy and understanding. But they may also tend to be clinging, dependent
persons, unable to make their own decisions, or unwilling
to try.

Physical troubles in this sign are all connected with the
digestive tract: There are possibilities of ulcers, dysentery,
diarrhoea, dyspepsia, and an inclination to obesity.

Note: Several astrologers maintain that the Moon in Cancer
is connected with carcinoma (cancer) of the stomach or
breast. My own view is that medical knowledge of this
dreadful disease is not yet well advanced enough to make
any such pronouncements. I fear that some astrologers are
too quick to link the sign Cancer with the disease cancer,
merely because of a coincidence of names. But if we trace
the etymologies of these names, they bear no relation at all.
As we've seen, the *sign* is called Cancer because that is the
name of one hard-shelled water-creature, which the Greeks
called The Tortoise and we call The Crab. The *disease* is
called cancer not because it has anything to do with the
stars or hard shells or aquatic life, but because some
tumours were once thought to look like crabs in shape, and
because doctors like to give diseases Latin names.

Since those born with planets in this sign are liable to
fret and worry, I feel it is irresponsible of any astrologer
to cause them more worry, unnecessary worry, on the basis
of an ignorant confusion of names. So far, no one can say
with any certainty whether any planet or sign has anything
to do with carcinoma. Despite medical and astrological research, this disease is still hardly more predictable than
lightning.

RISING SIGN: Those born with Cancer in the Ascendant have
round faces, thin lips, frown lines, heavy necks and fleshy
jaws. Their short noses and flat cheeks make them almost
'moon-faced'. Their eyes habitually convey an expression of
sympathy and affection. The body type is *endomorphic*,
tending to softness.

CHAPTER FIVE

Leo ♌

Sun sign period: 22 July to 21 August
Ruling planet: The Sun ☉
   The Sun makes those it governs creative, generous, sociable and dignified. They have exceptional organizing and executive abilities, strong affections, and a love of children
Polarity: Positive or masculine (extraverted, active, stressful, 'type A' persons)
Element: Fire (enthusiasm, haste)
Nature: Fixed (enduring)

LEO, THE LION was called the Lion in Egypt and in Babylon, the Great Dog. Its constellation really resembles a heraldic 'lion couchant' or an Egyptian hieroglyphic lion. Mythical lions have always been characterized as kingly, noble, big-hearted creatures, from the time of Egypt's Old Kingdom (when the Leonine Sun was associated with the heart) to the Middle Ages and Richard Cœur de Lion. Leo rules the heart, the dorsal vertebrae of the spine, and the gall bladder. By reflex to Aquarius, it reacts upon the circulatory system.

SUN SIGN: Leos are bossy and domineering – and likeable in spite of it. They are forever organizing the lives of those around them, but usually with perfectly generous, altruistic motives. The fact is, a Leo cares about people, and feels that his concern gives him a right to run their affairs for them. At times this can be a valuable trait: Executives and generals, for example, are at their best when they are natives of this sign. But a Leo finds it hard to take orders from anyone he considers less competent than himself, and he

99

tends to rebel. Leo is the sign of both rulers and revolutionaries.

If you are born with the Sun in Leo, you are probably a generous, creative, enthusiastic person, an excellent organizer with a flair for drama and a desire to show off. You are especially capable at handling children, whether as a teacher or parent, and you may not be bad at commanding adults, either.

Leos have an unfortunate tendency to be dogmatic and opinionated, they may bully or bluster to get their way, and they may be snobs. They seldom have much patience with those holding contrary opinions, they patronize subordinates, and they tend to think rather too well of themselves. They are susceptible to flattery.

Unlike real lions, Leos are not lazy. They work hard, and often know how to get others to work hard for their cause. They love luxury, and habitually spend a lot on clothes, jewellery, cars and ostentatious living. But they also worry about the welfare of others, and are often found organizing charity work or government relief projects.

Leos are by nature the most stressful, or 'type A' persons. They enjoy taking on heaps of responsibility, solving other people's problems, and tackling executive difficulties. The penalty they pay is often some disease of overwork and stress, such as a heart ailment.

Symptoms and diseases: Chest pains, palpitations, degenerative heart disease, rheumatic fever (affecting the heart), high fevers, back pains, slipped discs, spinal meningitis.

Diet: Your diet should contain plenty of protein, and, luckily, most Leos really prefer lean meat, milk, eggs, cheese and legumes to carbohydrates. Unfortunately, they also tend to like thick steaks with plenty of fat, butter, cream and cream cheese – all the foods richest in saturated fats. These foods, as recent research from Finland shows, cause the level of blood cholesterol to rise, and that in turn seems to cause premature heart and circulatory system diseases. The answer is to replace saturated fats in your diet with polyunsaturates, chiefly found in vegetable oils.

Begin by trimming all fat off meat, and perhaps eating less meat. Replace beef or pork with chicken or turkey; whole milk with skim or plantmilk; cream with yoghurt; cream cheese with curd or cottage cheese; butter with corn-oil margarine. White fish are an improvement over most meats, and nuts, peas, beans and cereals are still better. (An exception is coconut, which contains the highly saturated fat, palmitic acid – better for soap than food.)

Magnesium sulphate, your cell salt, can be found in nuts, citrus fruits, apples, figs, peaches, plums, cherries, lettuce, cucumbers and onions.

Leos are often social drinkers and smokers. Moderate drinking is probably harmless, but of course smoking is a dangerous luxury, especially for those vulnerable to heart disease.

Herbs: Bay Tree (*Laurus nobilis*), ruled by the Sun in Leo. Bay berries are said to be more effective than bay leaves; Culpeper describes dozens of uses: taken in treacle they ward off infection, help coughs, and help ensure regular menstruation. Mixed with honey they help 'megrim' (migraine). The oil of the bayberries is rubbed on to relieve back pains, rheumatic pains and sore or cramped muscles.

Borage (*Borago officinalis*), ruled by Jupiter in Leo. Used to clear the blood and strengthen the heart: the leaves, flowers or seeds are pressed, and their juice made into a syrup. The flowers were formerly candied and 'are good for those that are weak in long sickness, and to comfort the heart' (Culpeper).

Angelica (*Angelica archangelica*), ruled by the Sun in Leo. The juice, like bay, was used to ward off infection, but more often the candied stalks or roots (the 'angelica' sold at supermarkets today) were used to warm the body and comfort upset stomachs.

Rue (*Ruta graveolens*), ruled by the Sun in Leo. Culpeper's recipe is to boil the seeds with dill, drink some of this decoction and rub some on the chest, to relieve cough or chest pain.

Saffron (*Crocus sativus*), ruled by the Sun in Leo. Cul-

101

peper wrote: 'Saffron is endowed with great virtues, for it refreshes the spirits, and is good against fainting-fits and palpitation of the heart; it strengthens the stomach, cleanses the lungs, and is good in coughs.' But he advised against large doses: 'a few grains' is enough.

Celandine (*Chelidonium majus*), ruled by the Sun in Leo. The juice was formerly mixed with oil and used as an ointment for sore eyes.

Eyebright (*Euphrasia officinalis*), ruled by the Sun in Leo. According to Culpeper, taking the juice of this herb in broth was good both for the eyes and for brain function.

Camomile (*Anthemis nobilis*), ruled by the Sun. Tea made with the flowers is said to have a calming effect on people who feel irritable.

Emotional life: The Leo is loyal and affectionate but, of course, bossy. He or she tends to take the lead in love affairs, and to insist on making all the decisions in marriage. Usually a frank, sincere lover, the Leo is also a devoted parent.

Profession: Anything to do with organizing should appeal to the Leo, including company director, political leader, orchestra conductor, senior civil servant. His love of display and showing off might recommend him for acting, dancing or sports (either in solo sports or as team captain). Leos also choose work with children, especially older children, as a teacher or youth leader. Often they are drawn to professions dealing with luxury and display, from sign writers and muralists to jewellers and furriers. Of course the Leonine enjoyment of arranging other people's lives for them works well in all counselling and advising jobs, including psychology, social work, and astrology.

Biorhythm risk days: (explanation on p. 198)

P	E	I
+	c	c
−	c	c
c	−	+
−	−	−
c	c	+

Habits: Avoid stress, overexcitement, arrogance, snobbery. Try to develop patience, tolerance, humility and the habit of budgeting both your money and your psychic energy.

MOON SIGN: Born with the Moon in Leo, you are a good organizer, but may tend to be overbearing. Your strongest assets are your natural charm and exuberance, well worth cultivating. Warmth, affection and loyalty are normally associated with this lunar sign, but so are conceit and an inordinate love of luxury.

Lunar Leos are vulnerable to heart irregularities, diseases of the circulatory system, low blood pressure and backache.

RISING SIGN: Those born with Leo rising are of the *mesomorphic* body type, tending to muscularity. Broad shoulders are common, as is a thick head of hair. If genetic factors permit, the hair is red or gold. The eyes have a forceful, commanding look, being wide-set beneath a broad forehead and arched brows. The nose is often hooked, and the mouth and chin show strength and determination.

Virgo ♍

Sun sign period: 22 August to 22 September
Ruling planet: Mercury ☿
  Mercury causes those it governs to be clever, quick-witted, intelligent, versatile, good with languages and logic; nervous, quick of movement, flighty, glib, nosey and subject to nervous strain
Polarity: Negative or feminine (introverted, passive, 'type B' persons)
Element: Earth (practical, methodical)
Nature: Mutable (changing)

VIRGO, THE VIRGIN has a curious symbol taken from the Egyptian hieroglyph of a seated woman. Some modern astrologers describe Virgo as more or less a dried-up old maid. This is a rather sexist interpretation developed in the Middle Ages, and inaccurate. In the ancient world, Virgo was the corn maiden, ruling the harvest month (when, in Britain, some farmers still weave a few stalks of grain into a 'corn dolly' in her honour). Virgo rules the depths of the earth, and the depths of the human body: the abdomen and intestines.* By reflex, to Pisces, Virgo reacts upon the feet.

SUN SIGN: Typically the Virgoan is discriminating, honest, hardworking and tidy, with an analytical eye for detail and an unassuming manner. Born with the Sun in this sign you are probably highly energetic, willing to help others, and

* It may be only a coincidence, but recent medical research indicates that eating whole-grain cereals may help prevent intestinal cancer.

capable of handling minute routines or tricky details. Virgoans can also be fussy, they worry too much over small matters, and they tend to cling to convention more than they should. They have a reputation as harsh critics – or keen analysts – depending on the situation.

Tidiness and precision are usual Virgoan assets, and so is modesty, in every sense of the word. Virgoans seldom show off, and are sexually unaggressive. Often they're content to do all the work while someone else (a Leo, perhaps?) takes all the credit, though the sharply critical Virgoan usually has something to say about this.

Few Virgoans become known as great intellectuals. It isn't that they lack intelligence, for most of them have Mercurial cleverness. But they prefer leaving broad problems to others, while they concentrate on details. This aptitude for logic and completeness makes them ideal researchers, either in science or history.

The natural place of this sign is the Sixth House, associated with health and disease. For this reason, Virgoans are usually more concerned than others with health matters. They have a great dread of disease, and worry too much about their physical health. In most cases, this worry is groundless, since Virgoans are strong and tend to live to a ripe age. Of course, worry itself can generate real illness, especially diseases of the intestinal tract.

Symptoms and diseases: Diarrhoea, spastic colon, appendicitis, hernia, typhoid, colitis, infections of the peritoneal cavity (the abdomen), indigestion, various intestinal parasites, and blockage of the intestines.

Diet: Your diet requires nothing special, only wholesome food eaten sensibly. Unless you are suffering from colitis or an inflammation of the intestinal walls, or unless your doctor specifically advises against it, the bread you eat should be *real bread*, that is, whole-grain bread containing bran, and not just white sponge. The table below shows the difference:

Constituent of 100% whole wheat flour	Loss in white (patent) flour (%)
Bran	100
Protein	15
Sodium	100
Potassium	57
Magnesium	92
Iron	69
Copper	69
Phosphorus	80
B1	30*
B2	75
B6	75
Niacin	64*
Biotin	90
Folic acid	80
Pantothenic acid	100
Vitamin E	100
Amino acids	12

(Source: Medical Research Council Special Report No. 297, 1960)

* Actual loss of 100%, but synthetic vitamins added to restore part of loss.

Live yoghurt is said to supply beneficial bacteria to the intestinal tract, and this seems as good a reason as any to eat this nourishing, pleasant food. If you eat a balanced diet of meat, eggs, milk products, vegetables, cereals and fruits, you probably do not need a vitamin supplement. Virgoans have a habit of swallowing pills to allay their own vague fears of ill health; this is unnecessary and can be dangerous (eg, iron poisoning from high-potency iron tablets). The nutrients in fresh food may be more effective than pre-packaged vitamins and minerals, and there's no chance of overdosing.

Your cell salt, potassium phosphate, can be found in all whole grain cereals, especially wheat, oats and rye.

Herbs: Fennel (*Foeniculum*), ruled by Mercury. 'Fennel has always been regarded as one of the best remedies to aid the digestion, and has wonderful anti-flatulence properties.' (Petulengro)

Summer savory (*Satureia hortensis*), ruled by Mercury. Dried and made into a syrup, it was traditionally taken for gas pains or cramps.

Valerian (*Valeriana hortensis*), ruled by Mercury. The root, boiled with licorice, raisins and aniseed was used as an anti-flatulent. Greek valerian (*Polemonium ceruleum*) was used for headaches, nervous complaints and palpitations.

Mulberry (*Morus nigra*), ruled by Mercury. The ripe berries have been used for constipation, and the green berries, dried, for diarrhoea.

Southernwood (*Artemisia abrotanum*), ruled by Mercury. Used in former times for abdominal cramps. Culpeper and Petulengro both mention baldness treatments; the former wrote of burning the seeds and mixing the ashes with salad oil as a hair tonic!

Emotional life: Virgoans are quiet, modest, often chaste persons, in part because they find it difficult to express their feelings. Often they find themselves in a relationship with someone who takes them for granted or treats them with indifference, and as often they nourish a secret love for someone without being able to put it into words.

Profession: Secretaries are the embodiment of Virgoan qualities: neatness, precision, tact, an eye for detail and the ability to work in the background. Other jobs suited to this versatile sign include librarian, scientist (especially analytical chemist), inspector, gardener, pharmacist, doctor, nurse, watchmaker or teacher (dealing with younger children).

Biorhythm risk days: (explanation on p. 198)

P	E	I
c	+	c
c	c	−
+	c	−
−	−	c
c	c	+

Habits: Avoid getting upset over small things, pointless worry, and excessive criticism of yourself or others. Try to develop self-confidence, broader interests.

MOON SIGN: Those born with the Moon in Virgo may be extremely timid, worrying, nervous people. You may suffer from nervous indigestion, while remaining outwardly calm. Your memory is good, as is your capacity for analytic work. Lunar Virgoans are likely to take an interest in chemistry, pharmacy, herbalism, gardening or the medical profession. Likely diseases, if the Moon is badly afflicted, are dysentery, enteritis and chronic indigestion.

RISING SIGN: The face of one born with Virgo rising is round, the nose long and thin, the mouth well-formed. The broad jaw tapers to a narrow chin, and the high, rounded forehead is pronounced. The Virgoan Ascendant is likely to be clean, neat, quiet of manner, possibly a bit prudish, but essentially clever and practical. The body type is *ectomorphic*, inclining to slenderness.

CHAPTER SEVEN

Libra ♎

Sun sign period: 23 September to 22 October
Ruling planet: Venus ♀
  Venus encourages love, attraction, partnerships, the fem-
  inine character in both sexes; love of beauty, harmony,
  money and possessions; placidity, gentleness, artistic sen-
  sibilities
Polarity: Positive or masculine (extraverted, active, stressful,
  'type A' person)
Element: Air (intellectual and communicative)
Nature: Cardinal (enterprising)

LIBRA, THE SCALES has a symbol derived from ancient drawings of a pair of scales. It represents the balance-point of the
year (half-way around the zodiac from the first sign, Aries),
the beginning of autumn and the time of weighing and
reckoning. In physical terms it stands for the body's delicate
fluid balance system, maintaining each cell at a certain level
of acidity/alkalinity. Libra rules the kidneys and the lower
(lumbar) region of the spine. By reflex to Aries, it reacts
upon the head and brain.

SUN SIGN: The Libran, above all, knows how to express himself with tact, charm and eloquence. Librans are the diplo-
mats, judges and referees called upon in almost any kind of
dispute, because they have a deep sense of justice and fair
play, and because their desire for peace and harmony com-
pels them to try smoothing things over. Born with the Sun
in this romantic, idealistic sign, you probably enjoy a deep
appreciation of beauty and art, and you need harmonious
surroundings. You tend to fantasize at times, and to strive

for impossible ideals, but in your daily dealings with others you manage always to appear refined and diplomatic.

Librans may also seem indecisive, frivolous and gullible. They tend to flirt, to daydream and to waste their time vainly wishing things were better-adjusted to their own sense of a fair world. Indecisiveness is the penalty they pay for their fine sense of tact: The Libran can win an argument adroitly or lose it gracefully, but all too often he doesn't care which. There is nothing forceful about the typical Libran personality, and he can often be duped into believing in some idea or some person unworthy of his belief.

Tact often serves the Libran well and keeps him out of trouble, but it can go too far: He wishes to appear to each person as they'd like to see him, and this can make him appear at times slick, evasive or lacking real convictions of his own. One can compromise too often, even, as the Libran does it, in the interests of peace and harmony.

Harmony is the key to all Libran actions; the desire for it causes him to retreat from discord and quarrels, and to seek refuge in beautiful fantasies. Unfortunately these bear little relation to the troubled, discordant world the Libran often finds himself forced to live in. Stress affects him badly, and he may suffer from stress-induced diseases such as kidney disorders or lower back pains.

Symptoms and diseases: Those born under the sign of the balance may have real trouble with the body's hormone balance, easily upset in times of stress. In such times, the kidneys are one of the ways by which the balance is maintained: An excess of one or more impurities is passed off through the urine. Too many stressful situations put this system under a strain, leading to kidney and bladder troubles. Libran illnesses include diabetes, nephritis or Bright's disease, kidney stone, bladder infections, uremia, lumbago and skin eruptions (a sign of impurities in the body fluids).

Diet: Librans need most of all to have a pleasant atmosphere at mealtimes: Cheerful conversation on light, trivial topics; good food, attractive surroundings and music. Too often natives of this sign concentrate only on the food, helping themselves to rich gourmet specialities that appeal to the eye and palate but do little for the body. By all means, food should look and taste delicious, but that needn't mean *boeuf bourguignonne*, crab mayonnaise or profiteroles. A fresh salad, grilled lean meat, and luscious fruit can look and taste just as good, provided some thought goes into the buying and preparation. As a Libran, you may seldom have a weight problem, being more than usually aware of your own appearance. But when you do put on weight, gourmet cooking is usually the cause.

Your cell salt is sodium phosphate, helpful in keeping the acid/alkaline balance of your body. It is available in asparagus, beets, carrots, strawberries, apples, figs, dried fruit, whole-grain rice, corn, peaches, plums, cherries and almonds.

Your diet should include copper, from such sources as parsley, mushrooms, Brazil nuts, lettuce and radishes, and especially from raw butter beans. Copper aids in the formation of essential enzymes. Though copper deficiency is rare in man, animals suffering from it become anaemic and develop chronic diarrhoea.

Herbs: Dandelion (*Taraxacum officinalis*), ruled by Jupiter in Libra. Taken as salad or wine, or the leaves boiled in broth, this herb was believed by ancient herbalists to promote the flow of urine, flushing the kidneys. The common British name was 'piss-a-bed', and the French, 'pis-dans-lit'. The roasted roots make a delicious, caffeine-free coffee.

Golden samphire (*Inula crithmifolia*), ruled by Jupiter in Libra. Culpeper reckoned that this herb could prevent 'the stone'; in any case it was formerly taken (the flowers in syrup) as a laxative.

Pennywort (*Cotyledon umbilicus*), ruled by Venus in Libra. Formerly taken to suppress urine flow.

Pennyroyal (*Mentha pulegium*), ruled by Venus. A form of mint. Boiled and drunk to aid digestion; applied in a paste to clear skin blemishes.

Emotional life: Librans are of course wonderful partners,

from the point of view of other people: They are considerate tactful, warm and loving, and have a great need to be with someone. But Librans themselves tend to exaggerate this need, and to rush into marriage or affairs simply because they don't care to live alone. They marry early, and often regret it.

Profession: Diplomat is an obvious choice of profession for the Libran, who will do well wherever tact and sympathy are required: social worker, receptionist, hostess, maître d'hôtel, steward, salesman, anything that involves talking to clients. The natural artistic flair of the Libran suits him for fashion design, art dealing, the making or sale of musical instruments.

Biorhythm risk days: (explanation on p. 198)

P	E	I
+	c	c
c	—	c
—	+	c
+	—	c
—	c	—

MOON SIGN: You are friendly and easy-going, with a natural charm and poise that makes winning friends almost effortless. Probably you are attracted to music or poetry, and have some talent in one of these fields. You may have problems making decisions and, if the Moon is badly afflicted, you may even be fickle, finicky or far too self-critical. Lunar Librans suffer commonly from headaches, kidney pains, uremia or Bright's disease (nephritis).

RISING SIGN: Those born at the hour when Libra is rising have a clear skin, a deep, searching gaze, and a mouth that is wide and expressive. Other features are usually fine and regular. The neck is very often long and refined in appearance. The body type of Ascendant Librans is slightly *mesomorphic*, tending to muscularity, but tall and well-proportioned.

112

Scorpio ♏

Sun sign period: 23 October to 21 November
Ruling planet: Mars ♂
    Mars makes those it governs decisive, freedom-loving, brave, strongly sexed, energetic, aggressive, impatient, angry and liable to accidents and injuries
Polarity: Negative or feminine (introverted, passive, 'type B' persons)
Element: Water (emotional, intuitive, unstable)
Nature: Fixed (enduring)

SCORPIO, THE SCORPION is a Babylonian sign; the Egyptians used a venomous serpent in its place. The Scorpio symbol is a stylized version of both: a serpent with a sting in its tail. The phallic imagery of both ideas was derived from this sign's traditional aura of sexiness. Secrecy and danger are also associated with scorpions, and with this difficult sign.

Of all venomous creatures, the scorpion alone is not immune to its own poison. It could, if so inclined, sting itself to death. The Scorpio too has deep-running passions, sometimes venomous, which he can turn upon himself; he can be his own worst enemy. Scorpio rules the sex organs and bladder and the prostate in males. By reflex to Taurus, it reacts upon the throat.

SUN SIGN: Natives of this sign are highly imaginative, capable of deep, strong emotions and quick actions. You have a tendency to know what you want and go after it at once. Your judgement is good, and you are brash only when necessary, but otherwise subtle and persuasive. Scorpios

113

can also be jealous, stubborn and suspicious, secretive and spiteful.

Whatever the Scorpio does, he does with all his mind and heart, and he knows how to drive others to work for his cause. This sign is often characterized as the principle sign of sexual passion, but the Scorpio is passionate about everything: work, play, friendships, sexual encounters, politics, religion. Love and hate are strong in the Scorpio, who may be disappointed when others fail to live up to his strength of feeling.

The Scorpio cannot be tied down to a dull, routine job. He wants a challenge, an impossible task to perform or a hopeless battle to win. In this he resembles Aries, but Scorpio is more subtle, capable of laying secret plans, working indirectly and alone, and fighting on long after others have given up.

He can be a jealous, even cruel lover, in part because of his natural suspicion, in part because of his own ardour, which he expects to be returned in full measure. (It never is.)

He finds it hard to unburden himself to friends and loved ones, or even to professional advisers; it goes against his natural secretiveness and his desire to fight his own battles. Of course, a trouble unshared is a trouble that can cause psychogenic disease. Scorpios are vulnerable to diseases of the bladder, large intestine, prostate gland, and reproductive organs.

Symptoms and diseases: The immunity of a Scorpio to any disease is usually low; whenever a 'flu bug' is about, he's the one who gets it. By reflex to Taurus, Scorpios come down with throat infections of all kinds. Males are susceptible to prostatitis and hernia; both sexes to bladder malfunctions, venereal diseases, and inflammations of the reproductive organs.

Diet: Scorpios usually eat well, favouring gourmet dishes and rich foods abundant in animal fats. Often this causes no weight problems until middle age, but it may have other, less obvious effects. Natives of this dynamic sign normally eat more and burn more, but this also means the body must

114

rid itself of more toxins, via the execretory system and bladder.

Saturated (animal) fats in the diet should be replaced by polyunsaturates. This means trimming the fat from meat; grilling rather than frying meat; eating chicken and game birds instead of beef and pork; and using corn-oil margarine instead of butter. A high-protein diet should include lean meat, skim milk, cottage and curd cheese, yoghurt, nuts, eggs and legumes.

Your cell salt, calcium sulphate, can help maintain cellular resistance to disease. It is associated with epithelial tissue, the lining of the mucous membranes. Calcium sulphate is to be found in asparagus, onions, kale, garlic, watercress, mustard greens, cauliflower (especially if you eat the green parts too), leeks, radishes, figs, prunes, black cherries and coconut. Coconut should be eaten in moderation, however; it contains the saturated fat, palmitic acid.

Herbs: Sweet basil (*Ocymum basilicum*), ruled by Mars in Scorpio. Herbalists used to say that a tea made of basil, taken before going to bed, could stop a cold that was just beginning. We frequently use this delicious herb in cooking, but the ancients had many disputes about it. Some attacked it as a poison, while others defended it but would not say what its virtues were! Culpeper wrote: 'as it helps the deficiency of Venus in one kind, so it spoils all her actions in another. I dare write no more of it.' It sounds as though he believed it to be anti-aphrodisiac.

Wild Arrach (*Atriplex olida*), ruled by Venus in Scorpio. It was praised highly by Culpeper, who recommended mixing the juice with honey and taking it for feminine disorders, such as irregular menstruation.

Nettles (*Urtica dioica*), ruled by Mars. Boiled nettles produce a water that, mixed with honey, has long been used for sore throats and coughs.

Tarragon (*Artemisia dracunculus*), ruled by Mars. The leaves were formerly taken for diarrhoea.

Hops (*Humulus lupulus*), ruled by Mars. The leaves, boiled, or the seeds, powdered and put into drinks, were formerly taken to promote the flow of urine and to cleanse the blood.

Emotional life: You have a powerful, jealous love to give, and an enduring love, but if unreturned, it is likely to turn bitter. You are given to jealousy, and to brooding silently over your problems, then letting them out in bursts of anger or sarcasm. In marriage, Scorpios may have difficulty, unless they find the right patient, faithful partner.

Profession: Anything demanding research, solving mysteries or secret work, especially of a hard, taxing variety: psychiatrist, detective, policeman, butcher, undertaker, pathologist, soldier or almost any job in insurance or finance. Also, unfortunately, Scorpios seem to make successful criminals, especially if the Sun is badly afflicted in their chart. They also make good bank tellers, novelists and investigative reporters.

Most Scorpios become interested in the occult sooner or later. Their deep sensitivity may fit them to become spiritual healers or psychic mediums. But this is far more likely if they have the Moon in Arachne (see Chapter 13).

Biorhythm risk days: (explanation on p. 198)

P	E	I
c	+	c
−	+	−
c	−	+
+	−	−
−	c	−

MOON SIGN: Scorpio emotions run even stronger under the lunar influence, but so do pride and stubbornness. The lunar Scorpio can be moody or resentful, though he may also have a great personal magnetism, a subtle intensity of character that influences others. If the Moon is badly afflicted, however, he may be cruel or immoral. Lunar Scorpios suffer from bladder stones, hernia, venereal diseases, and irregular menstruation.

Note: Lunar Scorpios may well be in danger from poisons, including food poisoning.

RISING SIGN: Those born with Scorpio rising are, if genetic factors allow, dark and swarthy, with dark, penetrating eyes. There is almost a bulldog set to the jaw, which is full and determined. The brows are heavy, the voice strong, the nose is rarely straight (it may be either Roman or upturned). The upper lip is short and often noticeably folded. Body type: *mesomorphic*, tending to heavy muscle.

Sagittarius ♐

Sun sign period: 22 November to 21 December
Ruling planet: Jupiter ♃
  Jupiter endows those under its influence with kindness, joviality, optimism, compassion, loyalty, a sense of justice, breadth of vision and an aptitude for languages and athletics; but also with extremism, lack of caution, wasteful extravagance, lawlessness, conceit, blind optimism and a love of gambling
Polarity: Positive or masculine (extraverted, active, stressful 'type A' persons)
Element: Fire (haste, enthusiasm)
Nature: Mutable (changing)

SAGITTARIUS, THE ARCHER in the Greek myth was the wise centaur Cheiron. Cheiron came from a distant land; he was skilled in all sports and languages, a philosopher and a prophet. He became the teacher of Hercules, Jason and Achilles. Cheiron prophesied that Hercules would wound him accidentally in the thigh with an arrow, and that the wound would prove lethal.

Behind this story lies a certain reality: Centaurs were a Babylonian idea, and it was from Babylon that prophets, philosophers and priests went to Greece to teach their skills. And in all the countries of the ancient Middle East, the thigh was associated with sanctity and wisdom.* Sagittarius rules the hips, thighs, coccyx (base of spine), and the liver. By reflex to Gemini, it reacts upon the lungs.

  * For example, Pythagoras was said to have an artificial thigh of pure gold; Greeks burned the thigh-meat of an ox in sacrifice; and see also *Revelations* 19:16.

SUN SIGN: Born with the Sun in Sagittarius, you are probably unconventional, reckless, with a genuine love of knowledge and a desire to explore new territories and learn new languages. You are self-reliant, dislike taking orders or obeying restrictions. Honesty and outspokenness are usual Sagittarian traits, as are optimism and joviality. Sagittarians can also be prone to exaggeration, bluntness, tactlessness, blind optimism and irresponsibility.

Natives of this freedom-loving sign like to keep on the move, and they hate convention of any sort. They tend to dress differently, to enjoy unusual jobs, especially those involving a challenge or a chance to explore the unknown. Sagittarians often go in for outdoor sports, such as riding or driving; anything involving movement through open country. This same love of novelty and unknown places makes them good at academic pursuits, religious studies, philosophy and languages.

Note: Young Sagittarians are especially fond of fast, reckless driving, and so are likely to be involved in accidents. The injuries received tend to be located in the hips, pelvis or thighs.

The Sagittarian has generally good health, but tends to abuse it, chiefly by excesses. Over-indulgence in food or drink, over-exertion in sports, and heavy smoking are always risk areas for those of this hard-living sign. For this reason, perhaps, Sagittarians tend to suffer from diseases of the liver and circulatory system.

Symptoms and diseases: Fevers, piles, sciatica, rheumatism of the hip or thigh, hip fractures or dislocations, cirrhosis of the liver, hepatitis, liver malfunction.

Diet: Moderation must be the first rule in any Sagittarian diet. The use of alcohol and stimulants must be kept to a minimum, and the size and number of daily meals kept within reasonable bounds. You may find that your eating habits are very erratic: At times you tend to gorge, while at other times (especially while travelling), you either nibble or fast. Such extremes can lead to constipation and piles; more important is the fact that it can place a strain on all

119

body systems, including the liver.

Experiments have shown that fatty degeneration of the liver can be caused by diets deficient in the amino acid methionine. Sagittarians can combat this by making certain that their diet contains sufficient amounts of either methionine or choline (the product which the body manufactures from methionine). Methionine is present in all animal products, including milk and eggs, and also in rice, corn, Brazil nuts, cauliflower and turnip greens. The best single source seems to be Brazil nuts, which contain 25 per cent more than any other food.

The Sagittarian cell salt is silica, necessary for the proper function of muscle tissue. Silica can be found in the skins of apples, pears, plums and peaches, in figs, strawberries, prunes, parsnips, whole-grain rice, groats and oats.

Herbs: Bilberry or blueberry (*Vaccinum myrtillus*), ruled by Jupiter. Blueberry syrup is an old remedy for coughs and chest pains, as is a syrup made from:

Cranberry (*Vaccinum oxycoccus*), ruled by Jupiter. Culpeper also claimed the cranberry as an anti-emetic.

Sage (*Salvia officinalis*), ruled by Jupiter. Of many uses: a tea made with sage and lemon balm (to improve the taste) was said to help settle upset stomachs. The juice was taken in warm water for hoarseness. Leg cramps were treated by boiling sage and bathing the afflicted part in the lukewarm water.

Chervil (*Anthriscus cerefolium*), ruled by Jupiter. Chervil taken in food was Culpeper's cure for pleurisy.

English myrrh (*Cicufaria odorata*), ruled by Jupiter. An old remedy for rheumatic pains was to take a spoonful of the seeds each morning.

Fig tree (*Ficus carica*), ruled by Jupiter. Syrup of figs is one of the older remedies for coughs and sore throats; it is now a common laxative.

Emotional life: In an emotional relationship, the Sagittarian tends to look for intellectual as well as physical companionship. He needs his freedom, and can't stand being tied down or possessed; jealousy only drives him away.

Profession: Teacher, clergyman, writer, publisher, advertising executive, philosopher, lawyer, translator or interpreter, explorer, sportsman, racing driver, jockey, animal trainer or breeder.

Biorhythm risk days: (explanation on p. 198)

P	E	I
+	c	c
−	c	c
+	c	−
c	−	−
−	c	−

Habits: Avoid over-exertion, over-indulgence, careless driving, tactlessness. Try to develop thoughtfulness, responsibility, and honest self-criticism.

MOON SIGN: You are fluent in more than one language, a good speaker, optimistic, cheerful and independent. Reckless social behaviour may be a problem; so can driving yourself too hard, though active sport should appeal to you. You may have great intuitive powers and an almost uncanny knack of foretelling future events.

Likely diseases are gout, sciatica, hip injuries, and (by reflex to Gemini) asthma. Eczema is possible, and there is some danger from fractures of the femur or pelvis.

RISING SIGN: A rather long face, a slightly long, straight nose, large almond-shaped eyes which are very expressive. The chin is pointed, the lips full, and the brow arched. Fair hair is common to this rising sign. The body type is tall, long-legged, but tending to slight softness of outline, despite heavy muscularity. Basically *mesomorphic*.

Capricorn ♑

Sun sign period: 22 December to 20 January
Ruling planet: Saturn ♄
    Saturn governs those who are cautious, practical, thrifty, reliable, patient, slow-moving, trustworthy and self-disciplined. They may also be selfish, aloof, severe, cold, dogmatic, cruel or heartless. Saturn governs depression and chronic ill-health, but also long lives
Polarity: Negative or feminine (introverted, passive, 'type B' persons)
Element: Earth (practical, methodical)
Nature: Cardinal (dependable)

CAPRICORN, THE SEA-GOAT is symbolized by a drawing of a goat with curled horns. The Gilgamesh epic of Babylon tells of a mythical water-creature with horns, called Ea, 'the antelope of the ocean', and the Babylonians have left numerous representations of fish-rams or fish-goats, always with a horned head and a fish's tail. This symbolizes the dual nature of man: Like the mountain goat, he aspires to the heady heights (of ambition and status). But like the fish, he is also submerged in the depths (of conventional ideas and emotional hang-ups). The Capricornian shows this duality more than any other sign's Native, and shows also its physical significance: What the sea-goat really lacks is its climbing apparatus, that is, legs. Legs and knees are the vulnerable portion of the Capricornian body, for this sign rules knees, bones, skin. By reflex to Cancer, it reacts upon the digestive system.

SUN SIGN: Capricorn aspires. He is industrious, methodical

and ambitious; reliable, careful and prudent; has determination and discipline and a patient, humorous outlook.

Born with the Sun in Capricorn you are likely to make a good businessman, with just the right sense of how and when to take a calculated risk, when to ask for promotion, and how to move ahead socially. You may meet with many disappointments, but you are seldom discouraged and always willing to resume the climb to success. Unlike many others, you have dignity and a realistic sense of your own worth, which hardly ever lets you down.

Should you find yourself stuck in a humble position with no way to the top, you also know how to make the best of that. The Saturnine trait of self-discipline should help you manage any obstacle-course life places in your path.

On the negative side, many Capricornians tend to be pessimistic, even gloomy. Over-caution and conventional behaviour hold them back, and in trying hard to conform to the standards of others, they may become puritanical and drab.

It's been said that 'all Capricornians are born middle-aged'. Though this is an overstatement, it's true that the Capricornian sticks to convention instead of defying it, and seems old-fashioned in his speech, dress, habits or actions. There are times when prudence, caution and conservatism are appropriate, of course, but certainly there are times (especially in personal and social life) when it pays *not* to act like an octogenarian. The best that can be said for this Capricornian trait is that the Capricornian is sometimes born with the kind of wisdom that seems to come to others only late in life.

Mentally, Capricornians are purposeful, logical and serious – though many have a delightful sense of humour – and inclined to worry. They live longer than others, and usually their minds improve with age.

Symptoms and diseases: Age of course brings problems of circulation and digestion, and diseases of the bones and joints. Capricornians are peculiarly subject to age-connected illnesses. Arthritis and all diseases involving calcium depo-

123

sits (such as kidney or gall stones), are common in this sign, as are intestinal blockages and poor circulation. Skin symptoms such as 'liver spots' (not a sign of any importance), moles, excessive dryness of the skin and even small skin cancers have been connected with Capricorn. However, this is a basically healthy sign, if unafflicted by Saturn. Capricornians are natural worriers, and can worry too much about their health.

Diet: Highly-spiced foods, fried foods and meats cooked in rich sauces are a problem for the delicate Capricorn digestive system. The native of this sign may find that many of his bodily processes, such as the formation of bile, are sluggish, and not up to dealing with heavy gourmet meals. Elimination is also slower in Capricornians; this may be helped by drinking plenty of water between meals, especially one of the many excellent bottled mineral waters, such as Vichy, Perrier, Malvern etc.

The Capricornian diet should include plenty of protein (lean meat, fowl, legumes, cottage cheese and yoghurt), whole-grain cereals, and a balance of wholesome fruits and vegetables, which should be taken raw or as juices.

The cell salt of Capricorn is calcium phosphate, which helps the body make use of vital abumin. Albumin is the protein serum found in eggs and white meats; particularly easy to digest, it contains most of the essential amino acids. Calcium phosphate can be found in pigeon peas, brown beans, spinach, lentils, almonds, lean meats, whole-grain cereals, asparagus strawberries, figs, plums, bilberries, eggs, cucumbers and celery.

Herbs: Comfrey (*Symphytum officinale*), ruled by Saturn in Capricorn. The bruised root, boiled in water and added to milk, is a traditional remedy for coughs and chest troubles. Petulengro writes: 'Country people know this . . . by several names including "knitbone" . . . because of its properties in healing fractures and joining bones.'

Red beets (*Beta hortensis*), ruled by Saturn. According to Culpeper, used to stop menstrual flow and diarrhoea.

Quince tree (*Pyrus cydonia*), ruled by Saturn. The seeds,

boiled, make a gluey substance which Culpeper applied to mouth sores and sore throats. He used the green, astringent fruit to stop diarrhoea, and the juice as an anti-emetic.

Solomon's seal (*Polygonatum multiflorum*), ruled by Saturn. Another old bone-setting plant.

White mullein (*Verbascum lychnitis*), ruled by Saturn. The leaves, boiled with sage, marjoram and camomile flowers, provide a water that is said to be good for easing stiff joints.

Amaranthus (*Amarantus hypochondriacus*), ruled by Saturn. Culpeper claimed the flowers, applied to a nose-bleed or a cut, could stop the bleeding.

Heartsease (*Viola tricolor*), ruled by Saturn. Formerly used for lung inflammations and pleurisy, the flowers being taken in syrup.

Emotional life: The Capricornian is shy, and probably finds all emotional relationships difficult, unless Venus is well-aspected in his chart. He can be rather cool and calculating in love, and at times too conventional and unexciting.

Profession: Civil servant, mathematician, banker, politician, scientist, teacher, engineer, farmer, mineralogist, builder, administrator, surveyor. The Capricornian often goes for job security, and a chance to make slow, steady progress up the ladder. If all factors in his chart allow it, he is likely to become famous, at some level, rather late in life. Secure, routine work usually appeals to him, but occasional Capricornians try something unusual – like mountain-climbing.

Biorhythm risk days: (explanation on p. 1 98)

P	E	I
c	+	c
c	c	—
—	+	c
—	+	c
—	—	+
c	c	c

MOON SIGN: Reserve, caution and prudence are the usual characteristics of this sign, and the Moon may encourage

125

their development into aloofness, over-caution and austerity. Try to avoid sinking into depression or taking the gloomy view too often, as you may be prone to do.

You are able to influence others, and can be a bit of a very un-Capricornian show-off at times. Other indications in your chart will help determine whether you will achieve greatness, or whether a secret enemy will try to thwart your plans. In any case, you are a dependable, persistent worker, practical and able to advance through honest effort.

Lunar Capricorn diseases include rheumatism, psoriasis, digestive troubles, and skin eruptions.

RISING SIGN: Even young persons who have Capricorn ascendant are likely to have lines on the forehead; the face has a distinguished but unsmiling expression. Brows are often pointed, mouth and jaw are set and serious. The hair is often thin, in both sexes, and lobeless ears are common. The body type is short, and *ectomorphic*, tending to slenderness.

CHAPTER ELEVEN

Aquarius ≈≈

Sun sign period: 20 January to 19 February
Ruling planet: Uranus ♅ (traditionally, Saturn)
   Uranus makes those it governs humanitarian, indepen-
   dent, original, inventive, versatile and strong-willed;
   but also cranky, eccentric, perverse, rebellious, hating
   authority and determined to be different
Polarity: Positive or masculine (extraverted, active, stressful
   'type A' person)
Element: Air (intellectual, communicative)
Nature: Fixed (enduring)

AQUARIUS, THE WATER-MAN has an obvious symbol, waves.
The Babylonian origin was the god-with-streams, depicted
as a man pouring water from two jars; in Egypt this god
was Hapi, representing the Nile. Human diseases associated
with water include dropsy (oedema, or swelling of the
ankles) and difficulties with the circulatory system, such as
varicose veins.
   Aquarius rules the shins, ankles and circulation. By reflex to Leo, it reacts upon the heart (causing dropsy, for
instance).

SUN SIGN: The Aquarian is kind and likeable but not always
easy to know. He can be rather distant, and often his mind
is on distant horizons. Frequently Aquarians engage in
humanitarian activities, they are progressive, original
thinkers, often scientists or inventors, and take an interest
in reform.
   You value your own independence, and don't mind going
your own way in furthering some cause (political, religious

or charitable), even if it means losing friends. You are almost certainly an idealist.

On the negative side, Aquarians can be unpredictable, eccentric, rebellious, contrary, tactless, unconventional to no good purpose, or intolerant of the opinions of others. Born with the Sun in this creative sign, you are likely to have a scientific, analytical mind, capable of producing lively new ideas.

Aquarians have generally good health, but sudden reverses are likely if the Sun is badly afflicted.

Note: There is some risk of accidents involving electricity, explosions or drugs, for almost all Aquarians. These accidents would include: *Electricity*: careless handling or misuse of electrical appliances at home or at work, wiring mistakes, lack of proper grounding (earthing), lack of fuses, overloads, short circuits; *Explosions*: mishandling of explosives, fireworks, guns, attempts to burn explosive material such as petrol, benzine, or spray canisters, gas stove accidents; *Drugs*: mistakes caused by addiction or illegal drug use, taking prescription drugs in wrong dosages, use of 'leftover' drugs from earlier prescriptions, taking drugs prescribed for someone else.

Symptoms and diseases: It is not uncommon for Aquarians to suffer from some vague illness, a kind of miasma that doctors may have trouble treating or even identifying. Just as often, however, such an illness may pass off as quickly as it came on, for no apparent reason. In some cases, Vedic medicine (see p. 174) may have an explanation. Aquarians suffer from varicose veins, pains or swelling in the lower legs and feet, and leg cramps. If possible, avoid jobs which require a great deal of standing in one place (eg, dentist, hairdresser, barber, bank teller). Walking, however, should be good for you.

Diet: Aquarians tend to take little exercise, despite their excess of nervous energy. If you have a sedentary job, it is best to cut the calorific content of your diet to a reasonable level (2000 to 3000 calories/day, depending upon your height and build). This diet should include plenty of fresh fruit, and citrus fruits should be emphasized. Whole milk is an essential for Aquarians, unless allergies or extreme obesity prevent your taking as much as you need of this nourishing food. Milk contains not only calcium, but two factors which help your body absorb calcium: protein and Vitamin D. Since, in the normal adult, the bones lose about 700 milligrams of calcium daily, this is obviously an important part of every diet, and especially the diet of an Aquarian.

However, whole milk is not an 'ideal food' for everyone. It contains about 3 per cent saturated animal fats, which can increase the level of blood cholesterol. If this worries you, or if for any other reason you don't wish to drink milk, there are diet alternatives. The calcium-rich vegetables include beetroot, carageen moss, horseradish, spring onions, parsley, watercress, and especially spinach. It may also be necessary to supplement your diet with cod liver oil capsules, for Vitamin D. At the same time, you should eat an adequate amount of protein-rich foods: lean meat, milk products or eggs, beans, peas, lentils or corn. Whole-grain cereals should be eaten in moderation, for they contain phytic acid, which interferes with the absorption of calcium by the body. If you eat whole-grain bread, therefore, you should increase the amount of calcium in your diet to make up for the losses caused by the bread.

Your cell salt is sodium chloride, common table salt, and the most common salt in the human body. Sodium chloride is taken in and excreted in large quantities by all healthy persons; its functions include the retention of body fluids. Sea-salt is recommended in place of the commercial product, because sea-salt contains a proportion of other trace elements required for healthy tissues.

Herbs: Barley (*Hordeum vulgare*), ruled by Saturn. A good source of magnesium, required to prevent dry, brittle nails and hair.

Beech tree (*Fagus sylvatica*), ruled by Saturn. The leaves are traditionally used in poultices to clear the skin of scurf.

Fumitory (*Fumaria officinalis*), ruled by Saturn. According to Petulengro, gipsy girls with dark, oily complexions kept them clear by washing with whey in which this herb had been mixed.

Medlar (*Mespilus germanica*), ruled by Saturn. The dried, powdered leaves were once used as styptics. The fruit is rich in the minerals required to maintain a smooth, healthy skin.

Ground moss (*Lychen terrestris*), ruled by Saturn. Binding wounds with moss is of course an old custom. Culpeper's headache cure was to steep moss in oil, then boil the oil and cool it, and apply it to the forehead.

Emotional life: Aquarians may at times seem dispassionate and aloof, but they are nevertheless loyal, faithful partners. An Aquarian lives alone without being especially lonely, and even in the midst of his family, may require a certain degree of independence.

Profession: Scientist, writer, charity worker, astrologer, radiologist, inventor. Independence and invention are keys to jobs for natives of this sign, who hate to be labelled and like to present the world with surprises. They have a fresh, new approach to everything, and wherever they are found – from the electronics and aerospace industries to reform and revolution – they are usually far ahead of the rest of us.

Biorhythm risk days: (explanation on p. 198)

P	E	I
+	c	c
c	—	c
c	—	+
—	—	c
c	c	c

Habits: Avoid irregular eating and sleeping habits, putting off work, and wildly eccentric behaviour for its own sake. Try to develop tolerance, tact and sympathy towards those who don't happen to hold your progressive views.

MOON SIGN: Born with the Moon in Aquarius, you may have a flair for astrology or some other unconventional science, or your taste for the unusual may be expressed in eccentric dress or some out-of-the-way hobby. You're friendly, kindly and easy to get along with, though your love of independence could get in the way of meaningful relationships. Diseases associated with this lunar sign include poor circulation in the legs, phlebitis or varicose veins. By reflex to Leo, lunar Aquarians may suffer from 'dropsy', properly called oedema. This is swelling of the ankles and feet due to the accumulation of fluid in the lower limbs; it can be caused by weakness of the right side of the heart (ruled by Leo).

RISING SIGN: Those born with Aquarius rising usually have a friendly, open look about the face; men are often exceptionally good-looking, with regular features, a strong nose and a wide, well-shaped mouth. The jaw is not always well-defined, and the face is usually longer than average. The body type is above average in height, tending to muscularity, *mesomorphic.*

CHAPTER TWELVE

Pisces ♓

Sun sign period: 20 February to 21 March
Ruling planet: Neptune ♆ (traditionally, Jupiter)
   Neptune gives to those it governs idealism, spirituality,
   imagination, sensitivity. They may be subtle, artistic and
   creative, but also deceitful, careless, sentimental, indeci-
   sive, impractical, unworldly and tending to worry
Polarity: Negative or feminine (introverted, passive, 'type B'
   persons)
Element: Water (emotional, intuitive, unstable)
Nature: Mutable (changing)

PISCES, THE TWO FISH is symbolized by a partial drawing of
two fish joined at the mouth; these were originally the
Babylonian fish-goddesses Anunitum and Simmah, joined
by a thread and acting in unison. Pisces is the last constellation and sign of the zodiac, and the third dual sign: just
as Gemini represents the two lungs, and Libra the two
kidneys, so Pisces represents the two feet. In modern terms
its rule is said to be over the feet, body fluids and lymph
glands. By reflex to Virgo, it reacts upon the abdomen.

SUN SIGN: Born with the Sun in Pisces, you are likely to be
humble, compassionate, sympathetic, emotional and intuitive, impressionable and receptive. Pisceans can also be
vague, careless, secretive, gullible, weak-willed and impractical.
   Feet are for running, and in the case of Pisces, for running
away from problems. Pisceans tend to be escapists, fleeing
into the world of their imagination. This can work either
for or against them: Positive escapism leads them to cre-

ative work in the arts, especially poetry, acting and dancing. Negative daydreaming is a blind alley, of course.

You probably feel outside influences strongly. You are sensitive to the moods of others, understanding and sympathetic, and sometimes this sensitivity seems almost psychic. But you can also be fooled more easily than others, for you lack the grain of cynicism that might enable you to see through the hucksters and tricksters about you. You tend to take people at face value far too often, and so are probably in for some disappointments.

The flaw isn't always simple gullibility. When a Piscean likes someone (and natives of this sign find something to like in virtually everyone) he tends to overlook that person's faults, to set them aside and try genuine communication on a deeper level. The Piscean doesn't usually mind being conned out of money, for instance, by a spiritualist charlatan or a fake guru, because he realizes that a more meaningful exchange might also be taking place: even frauds sometimes speak truths.

Pisceans are self-sacrificing persons, who enjoy caring for the sick, helping old people, children and animals, visiting prisoners, and social work of all types.

Symptoms and diseases: Pisces rules the feet, and foot troubles of all kinds may be expected: flat feet, osteoarthritis of the toes, plantar fasciitis (pain in the heel), lymphatic oedema (swelling of the ankles and feet), ingrown toenails, painful callouses and ringworm. Those born within the first two-thirds of the Sun sign period (about 20 February to 11 March) may be low-spirited and physically weak, susceptible to severe colds and flu.

Diet: The Piscean may follow fad diets too often, and can actually fall into a state of malnutrition through mistaken notions of eating one or two 'miracle' foods exclusively. Remember that there is no single miracle food, and no dietary panacea that can solve everyone's health problems. Everyone requires a balanced diet containing proteins, carbohydrates, fats, vitamins and minerals. There's nothing wrong with dietary experiment, such as fasting or eating only one food, provided it isn't carried on too long.

Children and animals have no diet problems; they follow only one rule, eat what you like. Adult humans, perhaps Pisceans in particular, simply don't know what they like. Some foods are expensive or unavailable, others are heavily advertised, and still others are eaten out of habit, or in obedience to some current fashion. The result is that we consume great quantities of fraudulent foods, whose look and taste bear no relation to their value as nutrients. Such foods, like narcotics, only increase the appetite.

Pisceans can break the vicious circle not by resorting to instant miracle diets, but by trusting their own excellent intuitions. Eat what your body feels it needs, from among the basic natural foods: lean meat, milk, cheese, eggs, fresh fruits, fresh green and yellow vegetables and whole-grain cereals. Piscean instincts run deep and strong, and can, given a chance, direct sensible eating habits. Try a health drink to begin with: live yoghurt, fresh fruit, honey, egg white, wheat-germ oil. Or try steamed crab with a fresh leafy salad (seafood treats should appeal to Pisceans in particular).

The cell salt of Pisces is iron phosphate. Deficiency of this can cause anaemia. There are only two really safe ways to take iron without risking liver damage from too much iron: the first is to take tablets under medical supervision. The second is to take it from natural sources: calves' liver, lean beef, spinach, fowl, cockles and butter beans all preserve iron salts during cooking. Raw foods containing iron (which should not be cooked) include parsley, almonds, egg yolk, dried figs and apricots.

Herbs: Common Alder (*Alnus glutinosa*), ruled by Venus in Pisces. 'The leaves put under the bare feet galled with travelling, are a great refreshing to them.' (Culpeper)

Common water soldier (*Stratoites aloides*), ruled by the Moon in Pisces. Less well known than other herbs, but Culpeper claimed it was cooling, useful against hot painful swellings, such as sprained ankles.

Turnip (*Brassica rapa*), ruled by the Moon in Pisces.

'Contains sulphur, iron, manganese. Good for skin troubles, asthma, dropsy, rheumatism, catarrh.' (Dr J. A. S. Sage)

Rose hip (*Rosa canina*), ruled by Jupiter. Rose hips are an excellent source of Vitamin C, now thought to be an essential preventative factor against many illnesses. Their traditional use (as rose-hip tea or syrup) was for coughs and colds, and to settle the stomach.

Meadow-Sweet (*Spiraea ulmaria*), ruled by Jupiter. Culpeper used this against fever and diarrhoea. A tea made by infusing the flowers can be a good way of supplementing iron and magnesium in the diet.

Emotional life: Pisces is easily overwhelmed in any relationship, being submissive and all too easily convinced of the perfection of his or her lover. Basically romantic and a devoted partner, the Piscean is not too strong on the practical side of an affair or marriage.

Profession: Actor, novelist, poet or musician – many creative fields seem open to Pisceans; sympathy and understanding help them in becoming clergymen, social workers, prison or hospital workers, doctors, psychiatrists, nurses, anyone caring for children or animals. They may also work with the feet, as chiropodists or in the shoe industry. If psychic sensitivity predominates in the chart, Pisceans enter the religious orders, become spiritualists, healers or hypnotherapists.

Biorhythm risk days: (explanation on p. 198)

P	E	I
c	+	c
—	+	—
+	c	—
—	—	—
c	c	c

Habits: Avoid tendencies to drink to excess or to develop a drug dependency, indecision, anxiety, phobias. Try to develop some self-reliance, healthy scepticism, frankness, a wider circle of friends.

135

MOON SIGN: Those born with the Moon in Pisces are likely to have more trouble than anyone else in making decisions. However your psychic and intuitive powers are strengthened, you are gentler and more imaginative, if less practical, than others. You may have to fight against depression and discouragement. Likely illnesses are dropsy, cramps in feet, poor circulation, a weakness for drugs, psychosomatic ills, colds and coughs.

RISING SIGN: Those born with Pisces rising often have large, round eyes with a far-away expression, exceptionally fine features, a smooth oval face and a generous mouth. The chin is pointed and the neck slender. The white of the eye may show beneath the iris. Small hands and a flat-footed walk are common. The body type is *endomorphic*, tending to fleshiness, with round shoulders.

CHAPTER THIRTEEN

Arachne ⊕ *The Psychic Sign*

Sun sign period: 16 May to 12 June
Ruling planet: The Moon ☽

ARACHNE, THE SPIDER is symbolized by the Celtic cross ⊕
which is also the astronomical sign for Earth. You won't
find Arachne in standard books on astrology, or on the
'stars' page of your newspaper. Most living astrologers will
not have heard of it, unless they happen to have read my
Arachne Rising.[1] Like almost everything connected with the
psychic side of human nature, Arachne sounds mysterious,
improbable and irrational: Arachne is the thirteenth sign
of the zodiac.

Astrology began in Babylon about 5000 years ago. But
the zodiac of twelve signs as we know it is only half as old
(it first appeared in 419 BC). In earlier times, astrologers
used a thirteenth sign, not only in Babylon, but in Crete,
early Greece and pre-Roman Italy. It was known too among
the Celtic Druids of Northern Europe, whose empire
stretched from Turkey to Eire. And even in North America
(though no one can be sure how they learned of it), the
ancient mound-builders inscribed upon numerous stones
figures of spiders, marked with the symbol ⊕.

The zodiac of thirteen signs was suppressed by Imperial
Rome, as a piece of 'dangerous' knowledge. Those born
under the influence of Arachne were thought to be magi
and sorcerers, gifted with strange powers. The suppression,
it must be said, was successful: Today we have practically
forgotten Arachne's existence, except in a negative way:
People still suffer from arachnophobia (fear of spiders) and
trisdekaphobia (fear of the number 13).

137

'Strange powers' are no longer a taboo subject. The psychic world is open to exploration, and the explorers – parapsychologists – are mapping its *terra incognita* at a dozen universities around the world. ESP, 'mind over matter', 'second sight', and all such powers are undergoing serious scientific investigation.

Uri Geller spent a year at the laboratories of the Stanford Research Institute in California, bending metal by apparently psychic means, copying drawings kept in double-sealed envelopes, even receiving ESP messages through solid steel walls. The two physicists who studied him were completely baffled by his powers, to which they attested in a report to the scientific journal, *Nature*.[2]

The Dutch sensitive, Peter Hurkos, demonstrated similar powers in a New England laboratory, in tests lasting over two years.[3] At Oxford University, 1800 people took part in a test of mass ESP, with intriguing results,[4] while in the Soviet Union, as we'll see, members of the Academy of Science are looking into long-distance ESP.[5] Two doctors at the Maimonides Medical Center in New York feel they have achieved a successful test of telepathic dreaming.[6]

If we accept the word of such researchers that psychic powers are real, and if we accept that the stars can influence all human actions, then it makes sense to wonder how the stars affect psychic powers. According to a survey of over two hundred psychic persons, far more were born in Arachne's Sun sign period (16 May to 12 June) than at any other equivalent time of year.[7] A further analysis shows that, of those born at other times of year, far more than usual were born with the Moon in Arachne.[8]

Peter Hurkos was a Dutch housepainter until an accident at the age of thirty changed his life. He fell from a scaffolding and suffered concussion; when he awoke in hospital he possessed an unexplainable new power. Merely by touching persons, or objects belonging to them, he could pick up information about them.

One night a woman whose husband was missing came to ask Hurkos to help. Police had been looking for the man all night, without success, and they had been reassuring the woman that her husband was probably all right. Peter Hurkos was given a coat belonging to the man. As soon as he touched it, he knew the man had drowned, and exactly where. Following his map, the police found the body.

So began Peter Hurkos's career as a 'psychic detective'. He has now helped the police of six countries to find missing persons, stolen objects, kidnap victims, murderers. He holds honorary badges from American police forces, a card from the Paris police, and citations from Queen Juliana and Pope Pius XII. Las Vegas casino owners have given him another kind of tribute – by forbidding him to gamble at their tables! When the Stone of Scone was stolen from Westminster Abbey, Hurkos told Scotland Yard exactly where to find it.[9]

The Sun was in Arachne when Peter Hurkos was born. When he had his consequential accident, the Sun was in Arachne again.

Robert Leftwich, a sales manager from Sussex, may be less famous than Peter Hurkos, but his powers are equally phenomenal. As a schoolboy he found that he could memorize a certain passage, and then *will* the teacher to call upon him to recite it, rather than anyone else. As an adult, he developed the technique of 'psychic shoplifting', willing shop assistants to look the other way while he walked openly into the shop and took something. He took a friend along as witness, and he tried this particular stunt exactly one thousand times, just to prove he could do it. He gave the 'proceeds' of these expeditions to charity.

Colin Wilson, in his book *Strange Powers*,[10] describes other Leftwich feats, from clairvoyance to dowsing – even 'astral projection', or leaving his body at will, to travel to a distant place. This may sound almost too good to be true, yet there are many convincing accounts of astral projection. The most puzzling story concerns the poet W. B. Yeats. One day, while a student on holiday, he began thinking of a fellow student, intending to write him a message. The message was difficult, so he delayed writing it.

Two days later came a letter from the other student, who was hundreds of miles away. He had, he claimed, seen Yeats in person in the crowded lobby of his hotel. Yeats – or his astral self – had delivered the message.[11]

W. B. Yeats, like Robert Leftwich, was born with the Sun in Arachne.

Sir Alec Guinness was born with the Moon in Arachne. Once he warned the actor James Dean not to drive his new sports car or he'd 'be dead within a week'. Within a week, James Dean was killed in his sports car.[12] On another occasion, Sir Alec managed to sleep on through the ringing of two alarm clocks, and so miss his usual train to London. That train crashed.[13]

Arachne also seems to affect the actual timing of psychic events. On 19 November 1964, a Mr Freed of New Zealand was awakened by a brief but terrifying nightmare. He dreamed that his daughter Jane (who was then 1500 miles away, a violinist with an Australian symphony orchestra) was gasping for air, choking and smothering.

Next day the explanation was in the newspapers. During Mr Freed's dream, two musicians in Brisbane had been picnicking on a beach when they were caught by a sudden riptide and nearly drowned. It took rescuers an hour to reach Jane Freed with a lifeline. That night, the Moon was in Arachne.[14]

During one week in April 1966, Russian scientists tried an unusual experiment in long-distance telepathy. In Moscow, a researcher sat before a collection of objects. After a moment's hesitation, he reached out and picked up one of them at random, a screwdriver with a black plastic handle. Another scientist spoke into a phone: 'What's he holding now?'

Two thousand miles away in Siberia, a young man named Karl Nikolaiev began to concentrate. 'Something long, thin . . . metal . . . plastic . . . black plastic.' He could not name the object, but he knew exactly how it looked and felt. He went on to identify other objects in the same way: a barbell, a coil spring, playing cards . . .

During that week, the Moon 'transited' (passed through) Arachne.[15]

The Sun and Moon were both in Arachne on the evening

of 30 May 1935. Bernard Law (later Viscount) Montgomery was then in India, attached to the Staff College of Quetta. That evening his wife Betty noticed a peculiar feeling in the air, which their dinner guest, a Colonel Hawes, explained away as 'electricity'.

Mrs Hawes was not in India, but in England (at Farnborough, Kent). That same night she dreamed she stood on a rock overlooking a plain. The sky turned grey and the plain began to crack open, showing human faces deep in the cracks. A voice whispered to her, 'He's going to be all right.'

Next morning, the town of Quetta was destroyed by an earthquake, perhaps the worst in human history. At least 20,000 people perished in the first few seconds. But Colonel Hawes was all right.[16]

You may have wondered about strange, inexplicable experiences of your own: You're thinking of someone you haven't seen for months, when suddenly the phone rings and it's him. You somehow know that an innocent-looking letter contains dreadful news before you open it. You dream a conversation and then it happens, word for word. You visit a completely new place, but can't rid yourself of the feeling you've been here before . . .

Arachne may well have something to do with it. When the Sun or Moon is in Arachne, psychic experiences just seem to happen. And when they happen often enough to one person, chances are good that this person was born with Arachne prominent in his horoscope.

The easiest way to find out is to have your horoscope set up by a reliable astrologer, and then ask him to tell you whether any planet, of the Ascendant, is transiting this portion of the zodiac: 25° 23′ 5″ Taurus, to 23° 4′ 37″ Gemini. Normally astrologers attach no significance to this part of the zodiac. But in psychic terms, this is Arachne, the Spider. Those born with the Sun, Moon or Ascendant in this portion are likely to be psychic, compared with those born in any other (equal-size) portion of the zodiac.

Biorhythm risk days: (explanation on p. 198)

P	E	I
c	+	−
−	c	+
+	−	c
c	−	+
+	c	−
−	c	+

PART THREE

Planets and Aspects

CHAPTER ONE

The Planets

A complete list of the major bodies of the solar system would be as follows: Sun, Mercury, Venus, Earth–Moon system, Mars, the asteroid belt, Jupiter, Saturn, Uranus, Neptune, Pluto and the possible transplutonian planet, Vulcan and finally the comets. Astrology aside, it must be clear that not all of these bodies have significant gravitational or electromagnetic influence on Earth. Such influence must depend upon the size of the body, its strength of radiation, and its distance from Earth. The Sun would be important to astrophysicists, for example, because of its great size and strong radiation. The Moon would be important because of its proximity.

On the other hand, certain bodies would be unimportant. The asteroid belt (several thousand minor planets or asteroids, thought to be the remains of an exploded planet between Mars and Jupiter) is too diffuse to have a measurable effect. Pluto, likewise, is small and very distant, as are the possible Vulcan and the comets – their physical effects on the Earth cannot be measured.

Astrology operates on similar principles. Normally no account is taken of the asteroid belt, Pluto or any transplutonian bodies, while the Sun and Moon are of the greatest importance.

The effect of each planet depends upon its sign and House in the birth chart:

1. A planet *rules* one or two signs. When found in its rulership, the planet is said to strengthen the effect of that sign.

2. A planet is *in exaltation* in one sign. The planet's effect is stronger in that sign.

3. A planet is *in detriment* in one sign, and *in fall* in an-

other. The planet's effects are negative or weakened in these signs.

4. Two planets may be *in mutual reception* with one another. This means that each is in the sign ruled by the other. For example, Saturn may be in Taurus (ruled by Venus) while Venus is in Capricorn (ruled by Saturn). This is beneficial: Each planet works to stabilize and strengthen the best effects of the other.

5. A planet may be *angular*, that is, within 8° of the Ascendant, the Midheaven, the Descendant or the Nadir (the four cardinal points of the chart). This serves to strengthen the planet's influence (whether for good or ill will depend upon other factors).

The details of planetary influences in each sign and each House can be found below, under the name of each planet.

THE SUN ☉

Rules: Leo
Exaltation: Aries
Detriment: Aquarius
Fall: Libra

Key: Strength, vitality, the life force, birth, the heart, the spine, the right eye and the left brain hemisphere

The general characteristics of the Sun have already been discussed (Part One) and its associated diseases in the twelve signs have been given in detail (Part Two).

Diseases in the Houses (solar affliction):
1st: headaches, eye weaknesses, brain disorders
2nd: mouth sores, throat infections, eye diseases
3rd: liver malfunction, muscular pains
4th: heart diseases, anxiety
5th: skin diseases, intestinal disorders, miscarriages
6th: asthma, TB, colitis, lumbago
7th: headache, weight loss
8th: eye diseases, colonic infections, jaundice, urinary infections
9th: hernia, colds and flu, temporary sterility
10th: arthritis, rheumatism, leg pains
11th: heart diseases, digestive troubles, varicose veins
12th: asthma, eye diseases

146

THE MOON ☽

Rules: Cancer
Exaltation: Taurus
Detriment: Capricorn
Fall: Scorpio

Key: Instinct, intuition, birth, the digestive system, stomach and breasts, body fluids, nutrition, the sympathetic nervous system

The general characteristics of the Moon have already been discussed (Part One) and its associated diseases in the twelve signs have been given in detail (Part Two).

Diseases in the Houses (lunar afflictions):

1st: chills, lethargy, ear infections, pleurisy, asthma, and a prolonged birth
2nd: allergies, skin diseases, toothache
3rd: colds, ear, nose and throat troubles
4th: insomnia, pleurisy, anxiety
5th: general weakness, digestive troubles
6th: urinary infections, kidney stones
7th: kidney infections, sinusitis, dropsy
8th: stomach ache, diarrhoea, poor health in childhood
9th: ulcers, sciatica
10th: skin infections, accidents and injuries, arthritis
11th: leg cramps, dropsy
12th: anxiety and depression, uterine infections

MERCURY ☿

Rules: Gemini, Virgo
Exaltation: Virgo
Detriment: Sagittarius
Fall: Pisces

Key: Intellect, communication, brain (especially verbal functions), the nervous system, lungs and respiration

Since Mercury is nearest to the Sun, it never appears more than 28° from it in the chart. Mercury is the smallest true planet, less than half the size of Earth, and the fastest-moving planet (it orbits the Sun in eighty-eight days). Perhaps its quickness gave early astrologers the idea of associating it with nervous energy. Mariner 10 has shown us that Mercury has no atmosphere, but a densely-pitted surface like that of the Moon. Unlike the Moon, but like the Earth, Mercury is very dense, apparently packed with heavy elements. To the surprise of space scientists, Mercury has a magnetic field stronger than that of Mars or Venus. This means that it can affect electromagnetic activity here on Earth, including nerve activity – as astrologers have always claimed.

Diseases in the signs (mercurial afflictions):
Note: For Mercury's reflex action, read also the opposite partner of each sign (eg, for Aries, read also Libra).
Aries: vertigo, brain and nerve disorders, neuralgia
Taurus: stammer, lips, hoarseness, deafness
Gemini: bronchitis, asthma, pains or numbness in arms
Cancer: stomach ache, flatulence, hiccoughs, vomiting
Leo: back pains, palpitations, faintness
Virgo: diarrhoea, colic, shortness of breath
Libra: kidney pains, urinary disorders associated with 'nerves'
Scorpio: pain in bladder or genitals or menstrual troubles
Sagittarius: neuritis, pains in hip joint or thigh
Capricorn: rheumatism, pains in knee, gout, skin disorders (pruritis)
Aquarius: shooting pain in any part of body, rashes, varicose veins
Pisces: cramps in feet, memory defects, phobias

Diseases in the Houses:
1st: nerve disorders, chest colds
2nd: hyperthyroid over-activity
3rd: shoulder pains, neuritis
4th: angina pectoris (choking pain in chest)
5th: bilious attacks
6th: diseases of the skin, nervous rashes
7th: nervous impotence, sexual frustration, stomach troubles
8th: cramps, Parkinson's disease
9th: mental exhaustion
10th: eye diseases, hernia
11th: digestive problems, pains in any part of body
12th: temporary amnesia, foot pains, anxiety

VENUS ♀

Rules: Taurus, Libra
Exaltation: Pisces
Detriment: Aries
Fall: Virgo

Key: Love, emotions, harmony, throat, the kidneys, the lumbar region of the spine

Venus was recognized in ancient times as Earth's 'sister planet', and it is in fact the closest in size and the nearest planet to Earth. Moreover, Venus rotates on its axis so as to keep the same face turned towards Earth, each time they are closest together on the same side of the Sun. This indicates at least a gravity-relation between the two planets, and perhaps that they were once in contact. Venus is covered with dense yellow clouds that hide its surface from view, and that also trap sunlight energy (in a 'greenhouse effect') to heat the surface of Venus to about 900° Fahrenheit. The clouds are thought to be largely water. Oddly enough, Ptolemy said, long before telescopes and satellite probes, that Venus was a hot, moist planet.

Diseases in the signs (venereal afflictions):
Aries: head colds, headache, eczema of the face
Taurus: tonsillitis, mumps, goitre, diphtheria, and venereal diseases
Gemini: skin diseases, emphysema
Cancer: nausea, gastritis, obesity
Leo: spinal disorders, rheumatic heart disease
Virgo: colitis, gas pains, parasites (tapeworm, roundworm)
Libra: urinary disorders, kidney infections
Scorpio: prostate infections, irregular menstrual periods, syphilis
Sagittarius: hepatitis, cramps in leg and hip
Capricorn: shingles, skin eruptions, pain in knees
Aquarius: varicose veins, swollen ankles
Pisces: gout, fungal infections of the feet, gonorrhoea

Diseases in the Houses:
1st: urinary disorders, diabetes
2nd: bad teeth, mouth ulcers
3rd: asthma, deafness, ear infections, obesity

4th: heart diseases
5th: digestive disorders
6th: dyspepsia, renal infections, kidney stone
7th: anaemia, prostatitis
8th: eye troubles, requiring surgery (if Mars also afflicted)
9th: rheumatic complaints
10th: headache, bronchial colds
11th: arthritis, especially in hip or thigh
12th: eye infections

MARS ♂

Rules: Aries, Scorpio   *Key*: Aggression, energy, action,
Exaltation: Capricorn   muscularity, the red blood corpuscles,
Detriment: Libra   the adrenal glands, the kidneys,
Fall: Cancer   cuts and burns

The red planet Mars has always represented war and violence in ancient mythologies from every part of the world. Recent Mariner probes show that the planet itself has had an equally violent history: giant volcanoes (one 15 miles high and 370 across), lakes of burning lava, heavy bombardment by meteorites, raging rivers and wild sandstorms. The old mythic image still seems appropriate.

Diseases in the signs (martial afflictions):

Aries: cerebral haemorrhage (stroke), smallpox, brain fever, sunstroke, meningitis, insomnia, neuralgia, head wounds

Taurus: tonsillitis, diphtheria, swollen adenoids, mumps, nosebleed, acne

Gemini: pneumonia; wounds on arms, shoulders or hands; lung diseases

Cancer: tumours of breast or oesophagus, dyspepsia, loss of appetite, anorexia nervosa, gastric ulcer

Leo: muscular pains in back, heart attack, pericarditis, angina (chest pains)

Virgo: appendicitis, hernia, pinworms, colitis

Libra: nephritis, kidney stones, anuria

Scorpio: prostate infections, vaginal infections, excessive menstrual flow, haemorrhoids, scrotal hernia

Sagittarius: sciatica, fractures of the pelvis or femur

Capricorn: rheumatic fever, skin inflammations, chickenpox
Aquarius: fractures of the lower leg, blood poisoning, varicose veins
Pisces: foot injuries, corns, bunions, foot deformities caused by accidents

Diseases in the Houses:
1st: diseases requiring surgery, fever, brain diseases, piles
2nd: cataract, dental problems, tonsillitis
3rd: chemical imbalance, high level of blood cholesterol
4th: weak constitution, possible heart attack
5th: abdominal injuries, diseases requiring abdominal surgery, hepatitis, miscarriage
6th: blood impurities, injuries due to falls, cuts and burns
7th: headache, skin infections
8th: fevers, anxiety, appendicitis, danger from violence
9th: sprains of hip, inflammation of thigh muscle, pilonidal cyst
10th: chest pains, lung collapse
11th: fever, stomach flu
12th: infectious diseases, chickenpox (and formerly smallpox), skin diseases, inflammation of the eye

JUPITER ♃

Rules: Sagittarius, Pisces   *Key*: Health, optimism, expansion,
Exaltation: Cancer   joviality, the liver, the pituitary
Detriment: Gemini   gland, excesses
Fall: Capricorn

Jupiter is the largest planet of the solar system, weighing more than all the other planets, asteroids and moons put together. Yet it is light for its great size, being largely composed of hydrogen and helium. Physically Jupiter is a hot, expansive, highly magnetic planet.

In most ancient myths, Jupiter or an equivalent god led the pantheon of lesser deities. In fact, this planet has thirteen moons, more than any other. The god Jupiter sent down bolts of lightning; the planet Jupiter actually bombards the Earth with powerful radio waves that can interfere with short-wave transmissions – as lightning does.

151

In appearance, Jupiter is mysteriously beautiful, striped with red, ochre and pale blue. The biggest mystery about its appearance is the so-called Great Red Spot, first observed over 300 years ago. Over the years, some astronomers came to believe it was a landmark – but it moves North and South from time to time. Others thought it might be a cloud or storm centre – but it remains the same size and shape, being an oval 8000 miles wide and 30,000 miles long. At present, science has no certain knowledge about the Great Red Spot, or about the mysterious, shifting influence of this giant planet.

Diseases in the signs (jovial afflictions):

Aries: pyorrhoea, fainting, excessive sleep, vertigo

Taurus: tonsillitis, catarrh, boils, apoplexy, results of over-eating

Gemini: fatty degeneration of the liver, pleurisy, lung congestion

Cancer: hepatitis, indigestion from overeating, minor breast infections

Leo: palpitation, fatty degeneration of the heart, high blood pressure

Virgo: liver diseases, jaundice, severe fatigue

Libra: skin eruptions, kidney abscess, adrenal gland malfunctions

Scorpio: piles, urethral abscess, infections of prostate or uterus, skin disorders, sugar in urine

Sagittarius: gout, rheumatism, blood poisoning

Capricorn: eczema, hepatitis caused by obstruction

Aquarius: lumbago, lymphatic diseases, high blood pressure

Pisces: excessive perspiration, pain in feet, diseases caused by excesses of alcohol, drug abuse or over-enthusiasm in amateur medication

Diseases in the Houses:

1st: tendency towards liver, kidney, pancreas diseases, but this is generally thought to be the healthiest indicator of the chart. Great resistance to diseases

2nd: sore throats, pain in lower jaw

3rd: chronic indigestion, ear infections

4th: heart diseases
5th: jaundice, gallstones, dysentery
6th: generally normal health, possible eye or lung infections
7th: lumbago, weak bladder, sterility (temporary)
8th: fever, constipation, piles, low blood pressure
9th: herpes simplex (cold sores), skin irritations
10th: reasonably good health
11th: digestive disorders possible, but good health
12th: diabetes, eye infections, pain in fingers and toes

SATURN ♄

Rules: Capricorn, Aquarius
Exaltation: Libra
Detriment: Cancer
Fall: Aries

Key: contraction, depression, endurance, melancholy, slow changes, conservation of vital forces, the skin, teeth and bones; the gall bladder and spleen, rheumatism, ageing and illness

Saturn is the most distant and slow-moving of the visible planets. It takes over twenty-nine years to complete its orbit, never approaching closer than 837,000,000 miles to the Sun. It is the second largest planet and, like Jupiter, emits radio waves detectable here on Earth. Saturn is a cold planet, and its spectacular rings are thought to be composed of ice and snow. These giant rings – beginning 7000 miles from Saturn's surface, and reaching out another 41,500 miles – are only part of the satellite material orbiting this planet. Saturn also has ten moons, the largest (Titan) being larger than Mercury.

The influence of Saturn is said to be exactly opposite that of Jupiter, and it is from the names of these two planets that we take the words 'jovial' and 'saturnine', to describe human character. Saturn is called a *malefic* planet, associated with ill-health, pessimism, and melancholy. Yet it is also the planet of endurance, reliability, thrift – and longevity.

Diseases in the signs (saturnine afflictions):
Aries: dental problems, head colds, deafness, blood clots in brain arteries

153

Taurus: dental problems (lower jaw), chronic hoarseness, diphtheria

Gemini: chronic bronchitis, asthma, pulmonary tuberculosis, pains in shoulders and arms

Cancer: chronic indigestion, gallstones, loss of appetite, gastric ulcer, vomiting

Leo: hardening of the arteries, curvature of the spine, heart disease

Virgo: appendicitis, constipation, bowel obstruction

Libra: nephritis, chronic kidney disorders

Scorpio: sterility, hernia, constipation, piles, stopping of menstrual periods

Sagittarius: sciatica, gout, hip fractures in the elderly

Capricorn: skin diseases, rheumatism, arthritis, knee injuries

Aquarius: spinal diseases, slipped disc, sprained ankle, leg cramps, pernicious anaemia

Pisces: rheumatism, coldness or loss of feeling in feet, corns and bunions, chronic anxiety or depression

Diseases in the Houses:

1st: loss of weight, fevers, dental problems

2nd: glandular swelling in the throat, impacted wisdom teeth

3rd: chest pain, excessive perspiration

4th: pleurisy, chronic cough

5th: jaundice, miscarriage, chronic indigestion

6th: urinary disorders, fall causing bone fracture

7th: neuritis, haemorrhoids, liver complaints

8th: diseases of age (this being the classic indicator of a long life)

9th: sciatica

10th: rheumatic pains in hips or legs

11th: deafness, ear-ache, flatulence

12th: vague illnesses or symptoms, difficult to diagnose, often not cured, but (depending upon other factors), passing off spontaneously

URANUS ♅ (Modern planet, discovered 1781)

Rules: Aquarius
Exaltation: Scorpio
Detriment: Leo
Fall: Taurus

Key: disruption, sudden change, the circulatory system, physical changes, nervous breakdown, paralysis, cramp, eccentricity, body electromagnetism

Uranus is another giant among the planets, four times the size of Earth, and having five moons. While all of the planets have polar axes tilted slightly to the plane of their orbits about the Sun, Uranus goes further than most. It is in fact tilted over sideways, with its South pole pointing almost straight at the Sun (at one time of the Uranian 'year'). Since Uranus orbits the Sun in eighty-four years, but rotates on its own axis in sixteen hours, this makes for an erratic, wobbly sequence of days and nights.

Astrologers now believe Uranus to be associated with science, astrology, electricity, magnetism and especially with 'the unexpected' and sudden change.

Diseases in the signs (uranian afflictions):
Aries: shooting pains in the head
Taurus: injuries to the neck
Gemini: spasmodic cough
Cancer: hiccoughs
Leo: erratic timing of the heartbeat or pulse
Virgo: spasm of the abdominal muscles
Libra: injury from electric shocks
Scorpio: difficulties with physical changes during pubescence, pregnancy, childbirth, climacteric, menopause
Sagittarius: accidents involving loss of teeth, tetanus
Capricorn: meningitis, usually spinal
Aquarius: leg cramps, accidents from electricity or X-radiation
Pisces: cramps in feet, tetanus from foot injuries, claustrophobia

Diseases in the Houses:
1st: birth defects
2nd: sudden illnesses in infancy

155

3rd: sudden illnesses, accidents in childhood
4th: accidents in the home, adolescent illnesses
5th: sporting accidents
6th: hazards at work: electricity or explosives involved
7th: sudden stresses in marriage
8th: illnesses of age and senescence
9th: vivid nightmares, travel accidents
10th: stress diseases from career
11th: generally good health
12th: acute depression, agoraphobia (fear of the out-of-doors)

NEPTUNE ♆ (Modern planet, discovered 1846)

Rules: Pisces
Exaltation: Leo
Detriment: Virgo
Fall: Aquarius

Key: uncertainty, the mental and nervous processes, the thalamus, drugs and poisons

Neptune is slightly smaller than Uranus, and has two moons. Like Uranus, it is thought to have a clear atmosphere of methane and ammonia. Since it takes several years to transit a single sign, its influence must be seen as weak and diffuse in the charts of individuals.

Diseases in the signs (neptunian afflictions):
Aries: myopia, conjunctivitis, brain fever
Taurus: fear of suffocation, nervous laryngitis
Gemini: absent-mindedness, obsession, weak arms
Cancer: alcoholism, drug problems, frequent nightmares
Leo: high fever, delirium, heart ailments from drug abuse
Virgo: food poisoning, food allergies
Libra: rapid fluctuation in weight, rare diseases
Scorpio: fear of sex or sexual excesses
Sagittarius: religious mania, lung diseases
Capricorn: malnutrition, loss of body fluids
Aquarius: alcoholism
Pisces: involuntary trances, fungoid diseases of the feet

Diseases in the Houses:
1st: weak at birth
2nd: hard of hearing, weak memory

3rd: pleurisy, fear of drowning
4th: poisoning accidents
5th: anaemia, especially in puberty
6th: lethargy, danger of food poisoning, drug mistakes
7th: double vision
8th: depression from imaginary worries
9th: general good health
10th: fungal infections of the skin
11th: alcohol poisoning
12th: danger of alcoholism, drug addiction, vague fears and phobias leading to mental confusion

PLUTO ♇ (Modern planet, discovered 1930)

Rules: Scorpio   *Key*: regeneration, the unconscious,
Exaltation: (unknown)   elimination
Detriment: Taurus
Fall: (unknown)

Pluto is still, for most purposes in astrology, an unknown quantity. It was discovered in 1930 by Clyde Tombaugh, working with Percival Lowell. Many astrologers have made the serious mistake of attributing 'plutonian' features to this planet's influence, merely because of its name. Pluto was god of the underworld, so we find astrologers giving to this planet the rule of earthquakes, eruptions, volcanoes and big business (plutocracy).

This looks highly dubious, for two reasons. First, Pluto is not named after the ancient god, but after the men who discovered it: PLUTO is an acronym from *P. L*owell and *TO*mbaugh.

Second, the planet has appeared in only four signs since its discovery. It moves very slowly, transiting the zodiac in about 140 years. So its actual effects will require at least another century to become clear.

Everyone alive (unless over the age of 128) was born with the planet Pluto in Taurus, Gemini, Cancer, Virgo or (since 1971) Libra. Thus it may have global effects (some believe that its entry into Leo, in 1937, triggered World War II), but its effects in bioastrology are yet to be seen.

157

CHAPTER TWO

The Aspects

Exact formulae are not possible in astrology, which, like medicine, deals in tendencies and indications. Reading a birth chart is an art, depending upon experience and what the ancients might have called *gnosis*, but we might call 'a knack for it' – innate wisdom. But this too only shows with experience.

The planetary aspects in particular need careful study, for many of them have unknown or arguable effects. The list I have prepared here, after consulting several authorities,[1] is not meant to be either complete or accurate in every detail. Rather, it gives a general guide to good practice in bio-astrology.

The list is alphabetical, by disease or symptom. Under each is given one or more possible planetary aspects involved. Only the major aspects are given, in symbolic form:

Planet Symbols

☉	Sun	♂	Mars	♆	Neptune
☽	Moon	♃	Jupiter	♇	Pluto
☿	Mercury	♄	Saturn	A	Ascendant (rising sign)
♀	Venus	♅	Uranus	MC	Midheaven

Aspect Symbols

☌	Conjunction	0°	±8° orb, or allowance
☍	Opposition	180°	±8° orb
☐	Square	90°	±8° orb
△	Trine	120°	±8° orb

Note: The following list is not intended for use in self-diagnosis or self-treatment. Anyone who actually feels ill should, of course, see a doctor.

Abdominal migraine. (*See* Acidosis.)

Abdominal pain. (*See also* Acidosis, Appendicitis, Bilious

attacks, Colitis, Constipation, Food poisoning, Gall bladder, Gastritis, Gastric ulcer, Hernia, Indigestion, Ulcer.) This can be caused by virtually anything, from eating green fruit to appendicitis – or even by an ear infection. Check planets in Virgo (reflex: Pisces), ruler of the abdomen, or in Cancer (reflex: Capricorn), ruler of the digestive tract.

Abortion (miscarriage). This means loss of the developing embryo before the twenty-eighth week of pregnancy. Often there is no apparent cause.[2] According to Dr Jonas,[3] a woman born at Full Moon (☉ ☍ ☽) should not conceive when this pattern recurs.

Abscess. Pocket of infection anywhere in the body. ♃ ☌ ♂ □ ☽.

Acidosis. Excess body acidity. ♃ ☌ ♄ □ ♀ or ♂ ☍ ♃.

Acne. ♀ ☌ ♄ □ ♂ or ☉ □ ☽ or ☉ ☍ ☽

Adenoids. Lymphoid tissue, like tonsils, at back of nose. ♂ □ ♀.

Alcoholism. Check afflicted planets in Pisces. ☽ □ ♆.

Allergy. For rash, afflicted planets in Capricorn. (*See also* Hay fever.)

Amnesia. ☿ □ ☽ ☍ ♄.

Anaemia. Mars afflicted in Leo, by Moon or Neptune.

Aneurysm. A weak, 'ballooning' spot in an artery. Indications in Aries or Leo. ♃ ☍ ♂.

Angina. Chest pain. Afflicted planet in Leo.

Anorexia nervosa. Chronic loss of appetite. ♄ ☌ A □ ☽.

Apoplexy. (*See* Stroke.)

Appendicitis. ☉ ☌ ♃ □ ♂ or ♂ □ ♃ ☍ ♅.

Arteriosclerosis. Hardening of the arteries. ♄ ☌ ♃; ♄ ♂ ♀ □ ♃; ♀ ☍ ♅ □ ♃.

Arthritis. Saturn in the 6th House, afflicted by Mars. ♂ ☌ ♄ □ ♃; ☉ ☍ ♅; ♆ ☍ ♂ □ ♄; ☉ □ ♂ and others, too numerous to mention. It has been estimated that one person in twenty-five suffers from some form of arthritis at some time in his life.

Asthma. ☿ □ ♅; ☿ ☌ ♂ □ ♅ and afflictions in Gemini.

Athlete's foot. A fungoid infection. Neptune is often the afflicting planet, to some planet in Pisces.

Backache, chronic. This can have many causes, including

159

sprains, slipped discs, rheumatism, also malfunction of the kidneys or other internal organs. Where the spine is involved, the afflicted planet may appear in the sign ruling the portion of the spine: Taurus (reflex: Scorpio) rules the top seven vertebrae; Leo (reflex: Aquarius) rules the next twelve; Libra (reflex: Aries) rules the last (lumbar) five; and Sagittarius (reflex: Gemini) rules the coccyx or tailpiece.

Baldness. ♂ ☌ ♀ □ ♃.

Bilious attacks. (*See also* Cholecystitis, Hepatitis, Gastritis.) Various liver or gall bladder malfunctions come under this heading. ♃ ☌ ☽ □ ♄ or (☉ ♋) □ ♃.

Bladder. Scorpio (reflex: Taurus) rules the bladder, but bladder stones may originate in the kidneys (Libra: Aries), so check these for afflicted planet.

Bladder, gall. (*See* Cholecystitis).

Blindness. Eclipse, solar or lunar, in Aries. ☉ ☌ ☽ □ ♂ or ☉ ☌ ☽ ☍ ♂.

Blood disorders. Mars afflicted in Leo.

Blood poisoning. ♃ ☌ ♂ □ ♆.

Boils. (♃ ♈, ♉ or ♓ ☌ ☉) □ ♂. (*See also* Carbuncle.)

Breathing disorders. Afflicted planet, especially Mercury, in Gemini.

Bronchitis. ☿ ☌ ♄ □ ♂.

Burns. A planet in Capricorn, afflicted by Mars.

Cancer (carcinoma). Configuration unknown.

Carbuncle. A deeper, more serious type of boil. ♃ □ ♂.

Cataract. ☉MC ☌ ☽ □ ♄.

Catarrh. ☽ ☌ ♄ □ ♃.

Chickenpox. ♂ □ ♄.

Childbirth. Dr Jonas[4] claims a mother's natal Moon is important in predicting birth difficulties. But this is a complex subject, and more research is needed before configurations can be given with confidence.

Cholecystitis. Inflammation of the gall bladder. ♄ ☌ ☿ □ ♆ or ☿ ☍ ♆.

Cirrhosis of the liver. Jupiter is often the afflicted planet, in Sagittarius or Pisces. ♃ □ ♆ or ♃ ☍ ♆.

Colds. Afflicted planets for chest colds are in Gemini

(reflex: Sagittarius); for nose and throat colds, Taurus (reflex: Scorpio). ⊙ ☌ ♄, ☽ ☌ ♄, ♂ ☌ ♃.

Colitis. Inflammation of the colon. ♂ □ ☿ ☍ ♆.

Conjunctivitis. Inflammation of the eyelid. Sun afflicted in Aries, Leo or Sagittarius, while ⊙ ☌ A or ⊙ □ A or ⊙ ☍ A.

Constipation. Can have many causes, including improper diet, digestive or colonic disease, or worry. ♄ ☍ ☿.

Contraception. Dr Jonas's method of astrological contraception,[5] if it works as well as is claimed, is worth further investigation.

Coronary attack. (*See* Heart attack.)

Cystitis. Bladder infection. Afflicted planet in Scorpio.

Dandruff. Common, because it is common to have two planets □ in Aries (ruling the head) and Capricorn (the skin). ♃ □ ♂.

Deafness. ☽ ☌ ☿ □ ♄; ⊙ ☌ ♀ ☍ ♄.

Dental problems. Saturn in Aries (upper jaw), Taurus (lower) or Pisces (either). ♄ □ ⊙, ♄ ☍ ⊙.

Diabetes mellitus. Failure of the pancreas to secrete enough insulin to deal with sugar in the blood. ♄ ☍ ♃.

Digestive problems. Afflicted planets in Cancer or Virgo. ☽ ☌ ☿ □ ♄.

Dropsy. Accumulation of fluids in ankles and feet. ☽ ☌ ♀ □ ♃ or (☽ ♌) ☍ ⊙.

Dyspepsia. (*See* Digestive problems.)

Ear-ache. Afflicted planet in Aries or Taurus. ☿ □ ♅.

Eczema. Venus in Capricorn, badly aspected. ♀ □ ♅.

Emphysema. Loss of elasticity in the lungs, which remain partly inflated. ☿ ♊ □ ♅.

Epilepsy. Medical astrologers give many configurations for this disease, perhaps because it is old and common. Neptune is usually blamed, though perhaps (since one in ten of us carries the gene) heredity has more to do with it. ♂ ☌ ♆ ☌ ♃, Neptune afflicted in Cancer, or in the 6th House.

Eye diseases. Mercury badly afflicted in Aries may indicate diseases of the optic nerve. (*See also* Blindness, Conjunctivitis.)

161

Facial paralysis. ☿ ♈ □ ♄ or □ ♅.

Fever. Mars badly afflicted in any Fire Sign.

Fistula. Abnormal passage or abscess near the rectum. ☽ ☌ ♂ □ ♄.

Flat feet. ☉ ☌ A ♓.

Food poisoning. ☽ ☍ ♆.

Gall bladder. (For infections, *see* Cholecystitis.)

Gallstone. ☉ ☌ ☿ □ ♂; ♃ ☌ ♂ □ ♄; or Leo Rising.

Gastritis. Stomach inflammation, afflicted planet in Cancer or (by reflex) Capricorn. ☉ ☌ ♂ □ ☽.

Gastric ulcer. (♄ ♋) □ ♃.

Goitre. Enlargement of the thyroid gland in the neck, often because of a lack of iodine (eg, iodized salt) in the diet. ♀ ♉ ☌ ☉ □ ♆ or ♀ ♉ in the 6th House.

Gonorrhoea. ♀ ☌ ♂ □ ♄.

Gout. ♂ ☌ ☿.

Haemorrhoids. ☉ ☌ ♃ □ ☽.

Hay fever. ☽ □ ♅ or afflicted ☽ ♉.

Headache. Often, Mars afflicted in Aries. ♂ ☌ ☉ □ ♅.

Heart attack. Afflicted ♂ ♌ may predispose, but too many factors are involved to be sure. Possible links between sunspots and heart attacks (see p. 29 above) raise new questions, since sunspots are also linked to solar conjunctions with major planets.

Heart diseases. Afflicted planets in Leo.

Hernia, or rupture. ♀ ☌ ♂.

Hiccough. ♅ ☌ ☽ □ ☿.

High blood pressure (hypertension). ♀ ♌ □ ♂; ♄ ☌ ♃ □ ♂.

Hepatitis. Inflammation of the liver. ♂ ☌ ♃ □ ☽.

Impotence. ♂ ♏ ☍ ♄.

Indigestion. Jupiter afflicted in Cancer.

Insomnia. Mars afflicted in Aries.

Jaundice. Often from hepatitis (qv), or afflicted ☿ ♐.

Kidney diseases. Afflicted planet in Libra (reflex: Aries). ☽ ☍ ♄.

Low blood pressure (hypotension). ♃ ☌ ♄ □ ♂.

Laryngitis. ☽ ♉ □ ♂.

Lumbago, or low back pain. ☉ ☌ ♄ □ ♅.

Mastoiditis. Inflammation of bone behind the ear. ♄ ♉ in

12th House, afflicting ☽, also ♂ □ ♄.

Measles. ♂ ♉ ☿ ☍ ♄.

Menopausal troubles. ☽ ♉ ♀ □ ♄.

Menstrual problems. ☽ ☍ ♂; also ♄ ♏ afflicting ☽.

Migraine. ☿ ♈ □ ♆ or ☍ ♆.

Mumps. ♂ ♉ ♀ ☍ ☽.

Narcotic addiction. ♆ badly aspected to ☽, ♄ or ☉; afflicted ☽ ♓.

Nervousness. ☉ □ ♅; ☿ □ ♅; or ♅ afflicting ☿ ♊.

Nervous exhaustion. ☽ ☍ ♆.

Neuritis. ☿ afflicted by ♂, ♅ or ♆.

Nosebleed. Sometimes sign of hypertension. Afflicted ♂ ♉.

Obesity. ♃ afflicted in 6th House; ☽ ♉ ♃ □ ♅.

Parkinson's disease. Tremor, result of arteriosclerosis (qv). ♂ ☍ ☿.

Peptic ulcer. (*See* Ulcer.)

Peritonitis. Inflammation of the abdominal cavity, or peritoneum. ☿ □ ♂.

Phlebitis. Inflammation of veins in legs. ♂ ♉ ♀, ☍ ♀.

Piles. (*See* Haemorrhoids.)

Pleurisy. Fluid in chest cavity. ☽ ♉ ☿ □ ♂.

Pneumonia. ☽ ♉ ♅ ♉ ♂; ☽ ♉ ♆ □ ♄.

Prostatitis. Badly-aspected. ☉ ♏; ☉ ♉ ♄ □ ♂.

Psoriasis. ♂ ♉ ☿ ☍ ♄.

Rheumatic fever. Afflicted. ☽ ♌.

Rheumatism. (*See* Arthritis.)

Rupture. (*See* Hernia.)

Sciatica. Pain in the back and down the leg. Afflicted ☉ ♐; ☉ ♉ ☿ □ ♅.

Sinusitis, sinus headache. ☽ ♉ □ ♂; ♄ ♉ ♃ □ ♂.

Sleepwalking. ☽ □ ♆.

Smoking habit, tobacco addiction. ☿ ♊ afflicted by ♆ or ☿ ♓ badly aspected, but almost any planet in Pisces, if afflicted, can cause difficulty in breaking this habit.

Sore throat. Afflicted ☉ or ☽ ♉.

Sterility. ☉ ♉ ☿ ☍ ♄ or ♄ ♉ ♀ □ ☽.

Stone. A ♌ for gallstones; A ♑ with ♄ ♎ for kidney stones; A ♑ with ♄ ♏ for bladder stones.

Stroke. (*See* Apoplexy.)

Tapeworm and other parasites. A planet in ♋ afflicted by ♆.

Teeth. (*See* Dental problems.)

Tetanus. Infection often received through wounds. Afflicted ♂ ♉.

Tuberculosis. ☉ ☌ ♄ ☌ ☿ or ☉ ♊ ☌ ♄.

Tumour (benign). ☉ ♄ □ ♃ or ♂ □ ♃.

Typhoid fever. Afflicted planet in ♍ in 6th House.

Ulcer. Any open sore on the body. The sign of the afflicted planet depends upon the location: Peptic ulcers (in the stomach or duodenum) may have ♄, ♅, ♂ in ♋ afflicting ☉, ☽.

Urinary tract. Inflammations may be indicated by afflicted planets in Libra (reflex: Aries), or Scorpio (reflex: Taurus).

Venereal disease. Gonorrhoea, ♀ ☌ ♂ □ ♄; Syphilis, ☽ ☌ ♀ □ ♂.

Varicose veins. ♀ □ ♂; ♂ ☌ ♀.

Vertigo. Planet in ♈ afflicted by ♅ in the 6th House.

PART FOUR

Alternatives and Refinements

Other Viewpoints

No one astrological system can have the final word on health and the stars. Every tradition looks at the same problem from a different perspective, and solves it in a different way. That does not mean that some systems are wrong, but it does mean that all are incomplete. It's hard to see how any system could be complete, until we know everything there is to know about the stars.

So far we've been concerned with our own tradition, brought to its full development by Claudius Ptolemy about AD 200 in Alexandria. It draws on the ideas of ancient Europe, Babylon and Egypt, to produce a superb, workable method for understanding man in cosmic terms.

It is not, however, the only great astrological tradition. Vedic India, Han China and Aztec Mexico created their astrologies, equally ingenious, equally practical – but different.

Learning something about that difference can help us learn more about our own astrology. For that reason I've included a chapter each on India, China and the Aztecs. The chapters are brief, and make no attempt to explain everything about these peoples and their medical astrologies. Instead, they cover a few useful ideas of each: the Indian principle of 'shadow planets'; the relation of Chinese astrology to acupuncture; the Aztec 'calendar of health'.

A final chapter covers the more recent idea of biorhythms, an idea which is linked to the Pythagorean concept of stellar rhythms. Again, it is a kind of astrology – but different.

Some readers may be irritated to find conflicts and apparent contradictions between these various astrologies. Which,

167

they may ask, holds the 'right' answers about the cosmic factor?

It's a fair question, and impossible to answer. Think of how differently a house can be seen by different people: The architect is interested in its style; the historian in who lived in it; the builder in its leaking roof; the landscape artist likes its view; the banker thinks it a good investment, and so on. Who's right?

The universe is a house, too, but infinitely more complex. It would be foolish to ignore any view of it.

CHAPTER ONE

Vedic Astrology and Health

Ayurveda ('the science of life') is the ancient Indian discipline dealing with all health matters. It covers medical astrology, herbalism and many other esoteric systems almost unknown outside India.

The history of Vedic astrology is long, complex and not easily traced. We cannot say, for instance, which Western ideas first developed in India, or which were imported into India. But early Vedic practitioners did exchange ideas with the sages of China, the Persian magi, and the soothsayers of Alexandrian Greece. The holism that is Hindu science is made of many parts.

It would be impossible to outline Vedic astrology in one chapter – or even in one book – but some of its basic differences from Western astrology can be explained: the sidereal zodiac; the use of 'shadow planets'; the asterisms; and the 'saturated' birth chart.

THE SIDEREAL ZODIAC
In the Western tradition, the first day of spring begins the zodiac (0° Aries). Our zodiac measures a *tropical* (seasonal) year from one spring to the next. The seasons are not caused by the Earth's distance from the Sun, as some people may believe, but by the tilt of the Earth's axis. The axis is always tilted in (approximately) the same direction, so that as Earth orbits the Sun, there is a time when the North pole tilts towards the Sun (Northern summer), when it tilts away from the Sun (winter), and when the tilt is 'sideways' to the Sun (spring and autumn). The first day, or rather the first *instant*, of spring is the time when the tilt is exactly sideways; all over the Earth the days and nights are of equal length.

This *tropical* year is not only the basis of our zodiac, but our calendar. The first point of spring, 0° Aries, falls on 21 March in 1900, and it will fall on 21 March in the year billion. But it is not the only way of marking the year.

If the Earth's axis were tilted always at the same angle, the tropical year would also measure the time it takes Earth to complete an orbit about the Sun. Unfortunately, the axis has a slight, slow wobble, so that spring occurs before the Earth has gone completely around its orbit. This orbital or *sidereal* year is about twenty minutes longer than our calendar year:

sidereal year = 365 days, 6 hours, 9 minutes, 9·55 seconds
tropical year = 365 days, 5 hours, 48 minutes, 45·68 seconds

The sidereal year is important in any work dealing with the stars. It measures the true position of the Earth and planets relative to the constellations, while the tropical year does not. What this means for the zodiac is that our tropical version does not measure the true position of the Sun. When we say the Sun is in 0° Aries, we refer to the *sign*, and not the *constellation*. Actually at the first day of spring, the Sun is in 6° Pisces – and every year it is getting further from the Constellation Aries.

The astrologers have been arguing for at least two thousand years as to the relative benefits and disadvantages of the two systems. The tropical zodiac has the advantage of keeping the seasons, referring to all the seasonal life cycles on our planet. We know that Aries marks the spring, Cancer the summer, Libra the autumn and Capricorn the winter.

The sidereal zodiac, however, refers to the true position of the Earth in the universe. So there is something to be said for both systems.[1] Wisely, the Indian astrologers have kept both zodiacs, and developed formulae for converting one to the other. It is they who have worked out the 'Great Year', the period of time during which one zodiac cycles against the other, and the two will agree. This happens once every 25,785 years.

To convert a birth chart to the sidereal zodiac, M. K. Gandhi[2] gives the following formula:

1. Subtract 22° 9′ 19″ for horoscopes dated 15 April 1878 (or since).
2. Then subtract 4·2″ for each month since that date.

In other words, for a horoscope dated 15 May 1878, the total subtraction would be 22° 9′ 23·2″.

The result is a horoscope in the *nirayana* (sidereal) zodiac, used in Vedic medicine. It gives the true position of the planets at your birth, as shown on an astronomer's star map.

It also means your Sun sign may change. About four out of five people will find that, using the nirayana zodiac, their Sun signs differ from those they've always believed they were 'born under'. Ariens become Pisceans, Pisceans become Aquarians and so on. Someone who feels he is a typical Leo (sociable, commanding and dignified) may be disconcerted to find that his birth took place in the watery, emotional sign of Cancer.

Yet many Western astrologers, including the scholar Rupert Gleadow,[3] are coming to believe that the nirayana zodiac is a better index to the human character than the traditional tropical system. If you've wondered about this, or if you're simply curious to find out your own nirayana Sun sign (and check its accuracy in Part Two of this book), the following table may be used to find your Sun sign in the nirayana zodiac.

Nirayana		*Sun enters sign on this date*			
Sign	*1875*	*1900*	*1925*	*1950*	*1975*
Aries	12 Apr	12 Apr	13 Apr	13 Apr	14 Apr
Taurus	13 May	13 May	13 May	14 May	14 May
Gemini	13 Jun	13 Jun	13 Jun	14 Jun	14 Jun
Cancer	14 Jul	14 Jul	15 Jul	15 Jul	15 Jul
Leo	15 Aug	15 Aug	15 Aug	16 Aug	16 Aug
Virgo	15 Sep	15 Sep	15 Sep	16 Sep	16 Sep
Libra	16 Oct	16 Oct	16 Oct	17 Oct	17 Oct
Scorpio	15 Nov	15 Nov	16 Nov	16 Nov	17 Nov
Sagittarius	15 Dec	15 Dec	16 Dec	16 Dec	16 Dec
Capricorn	14 Jan	14 Jan	14 Jan	14 Jan	15 Jan
Aquarius	12 Feb	12 Feb	13 Feb	13 Feb	13 Feb
Pisces	13 Mar	13 Mar	14 Mar	14 Mar	15 Mar

In addition to the seven traditional and three modern planets of Western astrology, the Vedic system calls the lunar nodes 'shadow planets'. They are not in fact planets, but places where the Moon's path crosses the Sun's path. Eclipses can only occur at the two lunar nodes. If the Sun and Moon are at the same node, the Moon will pass in

Table of Lunar nodes, 1900 to 1981
(dates given are for entry of North node into sign)

Sign	Year	Month	Sign	Year	Month	Sign	Year	Month
♐	1899	June	♊	1927	May	♐	1955	May
♏	1901	Jan	♉	1928	Dec	♏	1956	Nov
♎	1902	July	♈	1930	June	♎	1958	May
♍	1904	Feb	♓	1932	Jan	♍	1959	Dec
♌	1905	Sep	♒	1933	Aug	♌	1961	July
♋	1907	Mar	♑	1935	Feb	♋	1963	Jan
♊	1908	Sep	♐	1936	Sep	♊	1964	Aug
♉	1910	Apr	♏	1938	Mar	♉	1966	Mar
♈	1911	Nov	♎	1939	Oct	♈	1967	Sep
♓	1913	June	♍	1941	May	♓	1969	Apr
♒	1914	Dec	♌	1942	Nov	♒	1970	Oct
♑	1916	July	♋	1944	June	♑	1972	May
♐	1918	Jan	♊	1945	Dec	♐	1973	Dec
♏	1919	Aug	♉	1947	July	♏	1975	June
♎	1921	Apr	♈	1949	Feb	♎	1977	Jan
♍	1922	Sep	♓	1950	Aug	♍	1978	July
♌	1924	Apr	♒	1952	Mar	♌	1980	Feb
♋	1925	Nov	♑	1953	Oct	♋	1981	Sep

front of the Sun, causing a solar eclipse. If they are at opposite nodes (180° apart), the Earth's shadow is cast across the Moon for a lunar eclipse. Ptolemy also considered these points important in determining body deformities or the likelihood of injuries causing permanent damage,[4] but Indian astrologers have made a systematic study of them.

The two lunar nodes move slowly backward (retrograde) through the zodiac. The ascending, or North node, is called in India *Rahu* ('the dragon's head'). It is said to rule diseases difficult to cure by normal medical means, including hiccoughs, parasites, hernia, snakebite and most diseases requiring surgery. Its afflictions in the signs and Houses are, according to Dr Chandrasekhar,[5] similar to the afflictions of Saturn (see Part Three).

The descending, or South node, is called in India *Ketu* ('the dragon's tail'). It is said to rule low blood pressure, parasites, fevers, stammering and malfunctions of the pituitary gland.[6] Its afflictions are similar to those of Mars (see Part Three).

Since the two lunar nodes are always 180° apart, the table on p. 172 for the North node (*Rahu*) gives the location of both. For example, when *Rahu* enters Aries, *Ketu* enters the opposite sign, Libra.

the table on p. 172 for the North node

ASTERISMS

Besides the larger structure of the constellations, Hindu astronomers studied the effects of smaller groups of stars in the zodiac. These smaller groups (usually of two or three) are called asterisms, or in India, *nakshatras*. There are normally twenty-seven nakshatras, though in some schemes a twenty-eighth was added, to make each of them govern one day of the Moon's travel. The Moon takes between twenty-seven and twenty-eight days to circle the zodiac, so that it passes near one nakshatra each day.[7]

According to Dr Chandrasekhar,[8] the duration of a disease can be predicted if, when the disease commences, the Moon's position is taken. Presumably this means *the duration if untreated*; otherwise this system produces the grim forecast that one person in seven who contracts any disease will die, which is surely wrong.

The nakshatras and their lunar positions and effects are given in the table below. It should be remembered that the positions are sidereal, so a nautical or astronomer's almanac should be used to find the Moon's position, rather than an astrologer's ephemeris. The extent of each nakshatra is 13° 20'.

173

Name of nakshatra	Begins at:	Duration of illness
1. Ashwini	0° ♈	1 day
2. Bharani	13 ♈ 20	Can be fatal*
3. Krittika	26 ♈ 40	9 days
4. Rohini	10 ♉	3 days
5. Mrigasira	23 ♉ 20	1 month
6. Ardra	6 ♊ 40	Can be fatal*
7. Punarvasu	20 ♊	7 days
8. Pushya	3 ♋ 20	7 days
9. Aslesha	16 ♋ 40	9 days
10. Magha	0 ♌	Can be fatal*
11. Purva phalghuni	13 ♌ 20	7 days
12. Uttara phalghuni	26 ♌ 40	15 days
13. Hasta	10 ♍	Easily cured
14. Chitra	23 ♍ 20	15 days
15. Swati	6 ♎ 40	16 days
16. Vishakha	20 ♎	20 days
17. Anuradha	3 ♏ 20	15 days
18. Jyeshta	16 ♏ 40	10 days
19. Moola	0 ♐	Can be incurable*
20. Purvashada	13 ♐ 20	15 days
21. Uttarashada	26 ♐ 40	20 days
22. Shravana	10 ♑	2 months
23. Sharavishta	23 ♑ 20	2 months
24. Satabhisha	6 ♒ 40	20 days
25. Purva bhadrapada	20 ♒	9 days
26. Uttara bhadrapada	3 ♓ 20	15 days
27. Revati	16 ♓ 40	10 days

* If untreated, or treated only by ancient methods available at the time this list was drawn up (*c.* 1700 BC).

THE 'SATURATED' BIRTH CHART

Western astrology has never solved the problem of why a person, known to be born with one sign rising (say, Leo), should nevertheless have some of the physical characteristics associated with another rising sign (say, the slight, active physique of a Gemini). This was the case with a friend of mine, born with 8° Leo rising and not a single planet in Gemini, who nevertheless seemed to be a Gemini Ascendant. I puzzled over his chart for some time, before discovering the ancient Hindu system called *navasama*. A method developed in South India, the navasama accounts for not only the rising sign, but the exact degree of that sign. For someone born with 8° Leo rising, the navasama position of the Ascendant is in fact Gemini.

This seems to explain why, among people whose birth times are known, only about <u>one in twelve</u> seems to fit perfectly the characteristics associated with his rising sign. Navasama seems to explain this as a 'saturated' birth chart: An extremely leonine person would have Leo Ascendant *and* the Leo navasama. I have not yet been able to test this system (mainly because it's difficult finding people who know their exact birth time to within fourteen minutes), so I present it here only as an idea. The table below gives the navasama position for every degree of every sign.

Degree	*Ari*	*Tau*	*Gem*	*Can*	*Leo*	*Vir*	*Lib*	*Sco*	*Sag*	*Cap*	*Aqu*	*Pis*
0° to 3°20′	♈	♑	♎	♋	♈	♑	♎	♋	♈	♑	♎	♋
3°20′ to 6°40′	♉	♒	♏	♌	♉	♒	♏	♑	♉	♒	♏	♌
6°40′ to 10°	♊	♓	♐	♍	♊	♓	♐	♍	♊	♓	♐	♍
10° to 13°20′	♋	♈	♑	♎	♋	♈	♑	♎	♋	♈	♑	♎
13°20′ to 16°40′	♌	♉	♒	♏	♌	♉	♒	♏	♌	♉	♒	♏
16°40′ to 20°	♍	♊	♓	♐	♍	♊	♓	♐	♍	♊	♓	♐
20° to 23°20′	♎	♋	♈	♑	♎	♋	♈	♑	♎	♋	♈	♑
23°20′ to 26°40′	♏	♌	♉	♒	♏	♌	♉	♒	♏	♌	♉	♒
26°40′ to end	♐	♍	♊	♓	♐	♍	♊	♓	♐	♍	♊	♓

NAVASAMA TABLE

175

CHAPTER TWO

Chinese Astrology and the Life Force

Astrology in China was never an isolated science or art. Like medicine, alchemy, natural history and philosophy, it was dedicated to the great search for immortality.

It is a 'great search' because immortality became the central concern of the two greatest philosophies of China, Confucianism and Taoism. Confucians believed that immortality could only be achieved through endless reincarnations. If a man is born into toil, poverty and disease, they said, he must make the best of his life, in the hope of earning a better place in his next incarnation. Taoists, opposing this view, argued that immortality is an inward state of being: paradise can be achieved here and now, because it lives within man. Through meditation and spiritual exercise, he said, man might achieve the Tao ('the Way', or true spiritual enlightenment) that would make him a living god.

In every sphere of life, these two philosophies battled for men's minds. In politics, Confucians were conservative, Taoists radical. In medicine, Confucians believed treatment to be a futile struggle against the inevitable; Taosists believed that without spiritual harmony, the Tao, treatment was useless.

In astrology, too, they carried on the battle. Confucians saw the endless cycle of stars rising and setting as a demonstration of the endless cycle of reincarnation. Taoists then pointed out that the stars, though they appear to move and change, are constant and eternal. Stars are not born and do not die, they said, because they are a part of immortal Nature.

This struggle between two major schools of thought might

have gone on forever, since there is some truth in each. In fact it lasted over 1200 years, and out of its disputes, the sciences of medicine and astrology were elevated to greatness.

These were old sciences at the beginning of recorded Chinese history, and before. Stone needles were used in acupuncture treatment as early as 11,000 BC,[1] and by 2358 BC astrologers were marking the seasons by constellations.[2] By the third century BC, the path of Jupiter was known, charted and used in predictions,[3] while Chinese physicians wrote enormous herbals, performed brain surgery and used vaccination and anaesthesia.[4]

The Confucian–Taoist rivalry, however, raised these sciences to the level of great arts, in the search for a key to immortality. Scholars generally agree that the highest culture in China flourished in the period AD 700–1000, which saw the invention of the printing press and compass, the writing of the great encyclopaedias, the establishment of the first medical school and much more. This golden age can best be characterized by two events, which, as we'll see, are not completely unconnected:

In AD 1027, the physician and teacher Wang Wei-i 'had a human figure cast in bronze on which were marked those points on the body important for acupuncture . . . The students practised with bronze figures in locating such points on the body.'[5] Twenty-seven years later, on 4 July 1054, astronomers at the Royal Peking Observatory saw a new star blaze into life. It burned brightly for over a year, then more dimly (though it can still be seen – it is the Crab Nebula).[6]

The point is not simply that astrologers and doctors of that era were making a detailed and systematic study of Nature, but that they were working for a common cause – the achievement of a harmony between man and Nature that would ensure eternal life. This harmony could only come about through a complete understanding of natural forces, including the force that brings a new star into being, and the pulse of life.*

* Diagnosis by taking the pulse rate was developed by the Chinese physicians at this time.

Chinese scholars classified their knowledge of the universe in two ways:

1. *Yang* and *Yin,* the two polarities. We have seen these already in Western astrology as the principles of activity and passivity, extraversion and introversion, masculinity and femininity, plus and minus. Yang symbolizes the positive, active, expansive nature associated with the Sun. Yin symbolizes the negative, passive, contracting nature associated with the Moon. All natural phenomena were seen as mixtures of Yin and Yang in various proportions, but so arranged as to preserve the overall balance of Nature.

2. *The five elements.* These correspond not only to the five visible planets, but to a five-part division of every natural phenomenon. The sky was divided into five parts: North, South, East, West and the Middle Kingdom (containing those stars which never rise or set). The human body too has its head and four limbs, the five senses, and ten major 'pulses' (energy meridians), five of which are Yin and five Yang. These meridians, the basis of acupuncture, will require more explanation, but first, a tabulated list of the five elements.

PLANET:	JUPITER	MARS	SATURN	VENUS	MERCURY
Element:	wood	fire	earth	metal	water
Season:	spring	summer	'ripeness'	autumn	winter
Colour:	green	red	yellow	white	black
Atmospheric influence:	wind	heat	humidity	drought	cold
Stage of development:	birth	growth	puberty	maturity	age
'Palace':	East (green dragon)	South (red bird)	Middle —	West (white tiger)	North (black tortoise)
Sense organ:	eye	tongue	mouth	nose	ear
Body structure:	sinews	blood vessels	muscles	hair	bones
Emotion:	anger	joy	anxiety	sorrow	fear
FU:	gall bladder	small intestine	stomach	large intestine	bladder
TSANG:	liver	heart	spleen	lungs	kidneys

As a reference guide to Western medical astrology, this list has its drawbacks: While Jupiter is associated with the liver in Ptolemy's system, and Mars might be said to affect the heart, other items are not so clear. Mercury (ruler of Gemini) ought to rule the lungs, while Venus (ruler of Libra) ought to rule the kidneys.

The reason for this disparity, however, is that this is not a list of planet rule, and the *Fu* and *Tsang* are not, properly speaking, organs. They are instead the ten meridians of acupuncture, said to be channels through which the vital energy, or life force, circulates through the body. The five *Fu* are Yang, or masculine, active meridians, running through five productive (but non-vital) organs. The *Tsang* are Yin, or feminine, storage meridians, running through five passive (but vital) organs.

Figure 19 shows the heart meridian. Acupuncturists believe that by placing needles under the skin at certain key nodes, the flow of vital energy can be stimulated, and a malfunction of the organ corrected.

It must be said that Western doctors seldom take this theory of meridians seriously. Having found no physiological basis for the meridians, they are inclined to dismiss the curative powers of acupuncture as dubious, and to speak of the Yin–Yang principle as 'gibberish'. So said Dr C. Norman Shealy, Associate Professor of Neurosurgery at the Universities of Wisconsin and Minnesota. Then he went on to say: '*But* there is another world of acupuncture – the world of pain – and here acupuncture is amazingly effective and I've used it with good results for years.'[7]

Acupuncturists traditionally have encountered many problems in locating the correct places for their needles, the nodes. Such diagrams as Figure 19 give only a rough idea, but only professional training and experience can enable the practitioner to locate these nodes exactly. Some acupuncturists have done it by feel, or by a kind of sixth sense; others, especially Westerners, make use of an electronic device measuring skin resistance.[8]

Oddly enough, Chinese physicians formerly used an electromagnetic device to locate the nodes. This was the astrological compass, shown in Figure 20, a device sensitive to fluctuations in Earth's magnetic field. It was said to measure

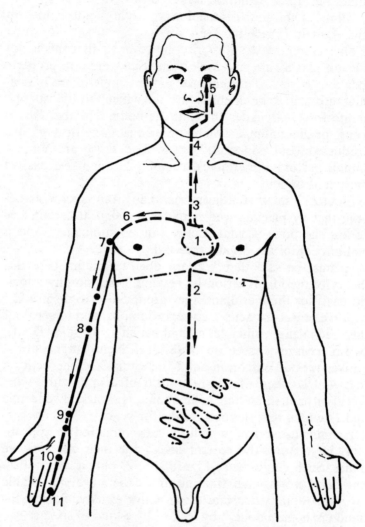

19. Acupuncture: the heart meridian. In traditional Chinese medicine, this is associated with Yin, the passive principle, and with the planet Mars.

flows of magnetic force within the Earth as easily as it measured them within the human body.

Chinese herbs are also classified by the five elements and two polarities. Since the great English herbalist Nicholas Culpeper classified herbs according to the Sun, Moon and five planets, his *Compleat Herbal* ought to show some correspondences with, say, the equally large *Pharmacopoeia* (*Pên-ts'ao-Kang-mu*), of Li Shih-chên.[9] In fact, the two works describe a great many natural remedies, giving the same planetary influence and the same application.

For example, Li Shih-chên, writing in 1578, lists tobacco (*Nicotiana tabacum*) as a cure for worms, and evidently includes it under Mars or the fire element. Nicholas Culpeper, writing c. 1640, lists tobacco as 'a hot martial plant', useful for 'destroying small worms'.

The following list gives only a few of the many herbal remedies mentioned by both Culpeper and Li, as specifics for similar ailments:

1. *Heart and circulation.* Asparagus (*Asparagus lucidus*); Mint (*Mentha*); Figwort (*Scrophularia*).

2. *Diuretics.* Garlic (*Allium sativum*); Horsetail (*Ephedra*); Mulberry leaves and bark (*Mora albus*).

3. *Cough remedies.* Angelica (*Angelica*).

4. *Styptics.* Peony (*Paeonia*).

5. *Restoratives.* Burdock (*Agrimonia*).

6. *Antiseptics.* Mustard (*Sinapis*).

7. *Anti-irritants.* Duckweed (*Lemna* or *Lens*); Self-heal (*Prunella vulgaris*).

8. *Digestion and stomach.* Sweet flag (*Acorus calamus*); Plantain (*Plantago major*); Dandelion (*Taraxacum officinale*).

9. *Endocrine system.* Sage (*Salvia*).

10. *Kidneys.* Water plantain (*Alisma orientale*); Peppermint (*Mentha piperita*).

11. *Asthma.* Mugwort (*Artemisia capillaris*).

12. *Arteriosclerosis.* Onion (one variety, *Allium fistulosum*).

THE CHINESE HOROSCOPE

Chinese astrology is a broad and detailed subject, and therefore outside the scope of this brief chapter. However, there

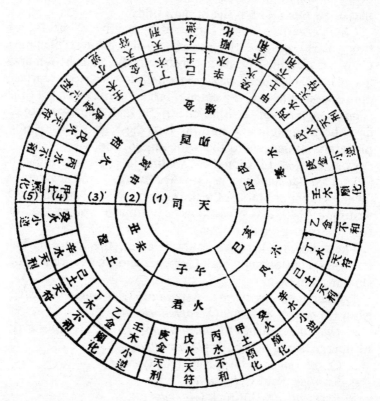

20. Astrological compass, used for both geomancy (the location of nodes in the Earth's magnetic field) and for acupuncture (the location of nodes of vital force in the body).

The diagram is taken from a reproduction of the work entitled *The Golden Mirror of the Art of Healing* (18th century AD).

On this astronomical compass the times of day, seasons and their interrelationships are shown as follows:

1. 'The Natural Order of Things' (innermost circle).
2. The twelve terrestrial cyclic signs and the division into hours.
3. The relationships of the five elements to each other, and their qualities.
4. The connection between the ten celestial cyclic signs and the elements.
5. The favourable and unfavourable constellations.

182

is space to mention at least the major feature of the Chinese horoscope, the twelve signs of the zodiac, and the years they govern.

Chinese astrology is based on a lunar year of 355 days, or twelve new moons (occasionally a thirteenth is added). Each year is named for one animal of the Chinese zodiac, and persons born during that year are said to have certain characteristics of their year-sign. Just as a Western astrologer may be interested in someone's Sun sign, a Chinese astrologer is interested in his Moon (year) sign.

To find your own Chinese Moon sign, see the table at the end of this chapter. Briefly, the signs and characteristics are:

The Rat: Charming, aggressive, opportunistic. If born in winter, there is a risk of imprisonment or accidents

The Buffalo: Quiet, patient, methodical, dogmatic. If born in winter, happy and less over-worked

The Tiger: Rebellious, reckless, a natural leader. Tends to push his luck and risk accidents

The Cat: Virtuous, refined, ambitious but usually happy. Cannot put up with discord and chaos

The Dragon: The sign of health and vitality. Courageous and idealistic, but too often tactless. Often finds true contentment late in life

The Snake: Intellectual, wise, often romantic, sometimes seems to possess a sixth sense. But lazy, and often jealous

The Horse: Popular, quick-witted, attractive, but selfish and hot-headed. For good or ill, these qualities are even more exaggerated in the rare sign of the Fire Horse (see table)

The Goat: Elegant, charming, fond of Nature but also a pessimist and a worrier. Craves security. As a young adult, may have a stormy emotional life

The Monkey: Sociable, fun-loving, mischievous, but also rather vain and arrogant. Unstable, likely to have family problems

The Rooster: Frank, bold and often courageous. But inclined to be a bit of a dreamer and a show-off. May have a rags-to-riches life, but just as likely a riches-to-rags period follows

The Dog: Introverted, stubborn, pessimistic, sometimes cynical. But a great humanitarian, and a confident leader. Life will be troubled for Dog born in the daytime, calm if born at night

The Boar: Innocent, gallant, trustworthy and tolerant. But also naive, inclined to be misled by others. If born near the beginning or end of the year, he will be more gullible than if born in the middle. May have difficult married life

Birth Table for the Chinese Horoscope

Directions: Find year of birth. (If birthday is before the day and month given, move up one row.) Name of year is at left.

Year of the:	Begins:		
Rat	31 Jan 1900	5 Feb 1924	10 Feb 1948
Buffalo	19 Feb 1901	25 Jan 1925	29 Jan 1949
Tiger	8 Feb 1902	13 Feb 1926	17 Feb 1950
Cat	29 Jan 1903	2 Feb 1927	6 Feb 1951
Dragon	16 Feb 1904	23 Jan 1928	27 Jan 1952
Snake	4 Feb 1905	10 Feb 1929	14 Feb 1953
Horse	25 Jan 1906*	30 Jan 1930	3 Feb 1954
Goat	13 Feb 1907	17 Feb 1931	24 Jan 1955
Monkey	2 Feb 1908	6 Feb 1932	12 Feb 1956
Rooster	22 Jan 1909	26 Jan 1933	31 Jan 1957
Dog	10 Feb 1910	14 Feb 1934	16 Feb 1958
Boar	30 Jan 1911	4 Feb 1935	8 Feb 1959
Rat	18 Feb 1912	24 Jan 1936	28 Jan 1960
Buffalo	6 Feb 1913	11 Feb 1937	15 Feb 1961
Tiger	26 Jan 1914	31 Jan 1938	5 Feb 1962
Cat	14 Feb 1915	19 Feb 1939	25 Jan 1963
Dragon	3 Feb 1916	8 Feb 1940	13 Feb 1964
Snake	23 Jan 1917	27 Jan 1941	21 Feb 1965
Horse	11 Feb 1918	15 Feb 1942	21 Jan 1966*
Goat	1 Feb 1919	5 Feb 1943	9 Feb 1967
Monkey	20 Feb 1920	25 Jan 1944	29 Jan 1968
Rooster	8 Feb 1921	13 Feb 1945	12 Feb 1969
Dog	28 Jan 1922	2 Feb 1946	6 Feb 1970
Boar	16 Feb 1923	22 Jan 1947	26 Jan 1971

* Year of the Fire Horse (once every sixty years).

CHAPTER THREE

Aztec Astrology and Life Cycles

They believe that the birth of men is regulated by the course of the stars and planets; they observe the time of the day and of the month at which a child is born, and predict the conditions of its life and destiny, both favourable and unfavourable. And the worst of it is, that these perverted men have written down their signs and rules and so deceive the erring and the ignorant.[1]

So did the bishop of Chiapas describe Aztec astrologers in 1698. What seems odd about his official horror, is that, only fifty-four years earlier, the Pope (Urban VIII) had been a practising astrologer! But the Spanish bishops were interested only in gaining converts, as the conquistadores were interested only in gaining gold, and so neither took much interest in Aztec culture.

It was the culture of a great and prosperous civilization, equal to those of Egypt, Babylon and China, and to our own. Our children set out the benefits and liabilities of our culture in the counting rhyme, 'Tinker, tailor, soldier, sailor, rich man, poor man, beggarman, thief, doctor, lawyer, merchant, chief . . .' Aztec civilization included all of these professions, for they are illustrated in the *Codex Florentino*,[2] along with many others.

The doctor is shown applying leaves to the back of a woman patient. It is impossible to say what the remedy is, or what it is supposed to do, for we have lost most of what we might have learned from Aztec herbal medicine. Until recently, Western science ignored Aztec ideas of herbal treatment, and only now is the remnant of our knowledge of these ideas being examined.[3]

What can be said, however, is that the doctor was trained in astrology. Astrology was of primary importance in med-

185

icine – and in all other professions – and almost no major decision in Aztec life was undertaken without consulting the stars. In medicine, it was important to know the date and time of the patient's birth, the date and time when the disease commenced, and the best date and time to pick the appropriate herbs and apply the remedy. All of these were determined by the motions and influences of the planets, as was the prognosis, or predicted course of the disease.

To develop accuracy in such predictions, the Aztecs of course needed the usual tools: observatories, written records and mathematics. Their observatories were great flat-topped pyramids, such as the Pyramid of the Sun in Mexico City. Most of these structures are decorated with calendars and elaborate calendric devices, in the Aztec hieroglyphic language. They are also built to incorporate in various ways the important numbers of Aztec astrology: *Four* (seasons); *five* (portions of the sky – as in China, the centre was added to the four compass points); *seven* (the visible planets including Sun and Moon); *thirteen* (the approximate number of Full Moons in one solar year) and *twenty* (the basis of the Aztec number system).

Thirteen and twenty became the most important numbers. Various structures were built with thirteen steps or decorated with twenty symbols. The pyramidal Temple of Tajin[4] incorporates 364 niches, thought once to have held the day-idols for an entire year. The number 364 was chosen rather than the true length of the year because 364 is divisible by thirteen.[5]

Our number system is based on ten probably because the Arabs who invented it counted on their fingers. The Aztec number system, based on twenty, probably began with fingers and toes. In any case, as we write *one, ten, one hundred* (ten 10s) . . . the Aztecs wrote *one, twenty, four hundred* (twenty 20s) . . .

But there is a deeper meaning behind their use of the numbers thirteen and twenty. It so happens that certain planet cycles can be marked quite accurately using these two numbers.

The Aztecs used a 'week' of thirteen days, not named but

186

simply numbered one to thirteen. They also used a 'zodiac' of twenty names of animals and objects. This was not a true zodiac, in the sense that it did not refer to constellations, but simply another kind of counting cycle (like 'Tinker, tailor . . .'). They used it to count days, weeks, months and years, and even eras.

Days were identified by both number and name, that is, using both the cycle of thirteen and that of twenty. This means that every day has a unique designation for a period of 260 days (13 × 20).

This may seem an arbitrary system, but it actually marked the movements of Mars and Venus. Mars was called Huitzilopotchtli ('Hummingbird Wizard'), a god of war.[6] Venus was Quetzalcóatl ('Feathered Serpent'), the god of wisdom and learning.[7] These two were chief gods, along with the Sun (called 'Smoking Mirror'), so obviously their movements were considered crucially important.* A meeting (conjunction) between any two of these luminaries would determine the basic rhythm of Aztec astrology.

Mars conjuncts the Sun every 780 days, Venus conjuncts the Sun every 585 days, and all three are in conjunction every 2340 days, on average. The conjunctions of Mars with Venus are more difficult to work out, because of their apparently erratic motion, but they follow this pattern:

(a) One period of about 97 days, then

(b) One period of about 169 days, then

(c) Three periods of about 689 days, then repeat (a), etc.

Amazingly, all but one of these six numbers is divisible by the Aztec week of thirteen days:

		Days	*Aztec* *Weeks*
1. ♂ ☌ ☉		780 =	60
2. ♀ ☌ ☉		585 =	45
3. ♂ ☌ ♀ ☌ ☉		2340 =	180
4. ♂ ☌ ♀	(a)	97 =	$7\frac{1}{2}$
	(b)	169 =	13
	(c)	689 =	53

* This makes sense in modern terms. Aside from the Moon, Mars and Venus are Earth's closest neighbours. Their powerful fields and rapid movements might be expected to have significant effects here.

Figure 21 shows how the Aztecs related the twenty names of their 'zodiac' cycle with parts of the human body.[8] The names and their explanations are:

A. *Crocodile*, the hieroglyph for breath. This rules the lungs, bronchial passages and larynx.
B. *Wind* rules the liver and pancreas.
C. *House* represents the 'home' of the living personality. It rules the brain and nerve functions.
D. *Lizard* rules the female reproductive organs, and female hormones in both sexes.
E. *Snake* rules the male reproductive organs, and male hormones in both sexes.
F. *Skull* rules the entire bone structure of the body, except the teeth.
G. *Deer* rules the right leg and foot, and the circulation of the blood.
H. *Rabbit* rules the left ear and sense of balance.
I. *Water* rules the skin and hair.
J. *Dog* rules the nose, sense of smell and sinuses.
K. *Monkey* rules the left arm and kidney.
L. *Grass rope* rules the intestinal tract.
M. *Reed* rules the heart.
N. *Ocelot* (or jaguar) rules the left leg and foot, and lymph glands.
O. *Eagle* rules the right arm and kidney.
P. *Vulture* rules the right ear and facial muscles.
Q. *Motion* (or earthquake) rules the tongue, taste and salivary glands.
R. *Flint knife* rules the teeth.
S. *Rain* rules the eyes and body moisture.
T. *Rose* rules the chest cavity, diaphragm and the breasts.

In the Aztec system, each day has a name from this cycle, and also a number from the cycle one to thirteen. The name gives the body part which may be predisposed to strength or weakness, while the number gives the indication of strength or weakness.

Using the calendrical system as known[9] and the information that the year 1489 was called 'Ten House',[10] it has been possible to reconstruct the Aztec calendar of health, at least provisionally, for our time. A few acquaintances of mine have tried looking up their birth dates, and found that this archaic system is still strangely accurate. I make no

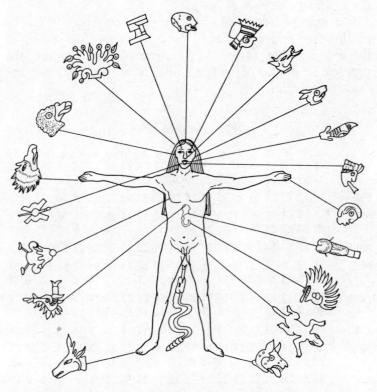

21. Aztec calendar of health. The symbols and their meanings are explained in the text. Beginning at the top and moving clockwise, they are: skull, rain, dog, rabbit, flint knife, crocodile, monkey, reed, grass rope, lizard, ocelot, snake, deer, wind, rose, motion, eagle, vulture, water and house.

claims for it, however, because it almost certainly lacks the subtlety of the original system (which also considered the hour of birth).

If you wish to check your own birth date in the Aztec

Health Calendar, you must find both the day's *name* and its *number*.

1. To find the *name*, use the two tables below: In the *first* table, find your *month and day* of birth. The small letter at the top of that column must then be looked up in the *second* table, under the *year* of birth.

For example, someone born on 12 February 1957: The small letter above 12 February is *c*, in the first table. In the second table, under '57', *c* corresponds to *House*, the sign for brain and nerve functions. Next, the day's number must be calculated.

Month and Day Table

	a	b	c	d	e	f	g	h	i	j	k	l	m	n	o	p	q	r	s	t
Jan	1	2	3	4	5	6	7	8	9	10	11	12	13	14	15	16	17	18	19	20
	21	22	23	24	25	26	27	28	29	30	31/	1	2	3	4	5	6	7	8	9
Feb	10	11	**12**	13	14	15	16	17	18	19	20	21	22	23	24	25	26	27	28/	1
Mar	2	3	4	5	6	7	8	9	10	11	12	13	14	15	16	17	18	19	20	21
	22	23	24	25	26	27	28	29	30	31/	1	2	3	4	5	6	7	8	9	10
Apr	11	12	13	14	15	16	17	18	19	20	21	22	23	24	25	26	27	28	29	30/
May	1	2	3	4	5	6	7	8	9	10	11	12	13	14	15	16	17	18	19	20
	21	22	23	24	25	26	27	28	29	30	31/	1	2	3	4	5	6	7	8	9
June	10	11	12	13	14	15	16	17	18	19	20	21	22	23	24	25	26	27	28	29
	30/	1	2	3	4	5	6	7	8	9	10	11	12	13	14	15	16	17	18	19
July	20	21	22	23	24	25	26	27	28	29	30	31/	1	2	3	4	5	6	7	8
Aug	9	10	11	12	13	14	15	16	17	18	19	20	21	22	23	24	25	26	27	28
	29	30	31/	1	2	3	4	5	6	7	8	9	10	11	12	13	14	15	16	17
Sep	18	19	20	21	22	23	24	25	26	27	28	29	30/	1	2	3	4	5	6	7
Oct	8	9	10	11	12	13	14	15	16	17	18	19	20	21	22	23	24	25	26	27
	28	29	30	31/	1	2	3	4	5	6	7	8	9	10	11	12	13	14	15	16
Nov	17	18	19	20	21	22	23	24	25	26	27	28	29	30/	1	2	3	4	5	6
Dec	7	8	9	10	11	12	13	14	15	16	17	18	19	20	21	22	23	24	25	26
	27	28	29	30	31/															
	a	b	c	d	e	f	g	h	i	j	k	l	m	n	o	p	q	r	s	t

Year of Birth (19..)

Name	01 65	02 66	03 67	04 68	05 69	06 70	07 71	08 72	09 73	10 74	11 75	12 76	13 77	14 78	15 79	16 80
(17 33 49)	17 33 49	18 34 50	19 35 51	20 36 52	21 37 53	22 38 54	23 39 55	24 40 56	25 41 57	26 42 58	27 43 59	28 44 60	29 45 61	30 46 62	31 47 63	32 48 64
Crocodile	a	p	k	f	a	p	k	f	a	p	k	f	a	p	k	f
Wind	b	q	l	g	b	q	l	g	b	q	l	g	b	q	l	g
House	c	r	m	h	c	r	m	h	c	r	m	h	c	r	m	h
Lizard	d	s	n	i	d	s	n	i	d	s	n	i	d	s	n	i
Snake	e	t	o	j	e	t	o	j	e	t	o	j	e	t	o	j
Skull	f	a	p	k	f	a	p	k	f	a	p	k	f	a	p	k
Deer	g	b	q	l	g	b	q	l	g	b	q	l	g	b	q	l
Rabbit	h	c	r	m	h	c	r	m	h	c	r	m	h	c	r	m
Water	i	d	s	n	i	d	s	n	i	d	s	n	i	d	s	n
Dog	j	e	t	o	j	e	t	o	j	e	t	o	j	e	t	o
Monkey	k	f	a	p	k	f	a	p	k	f	a	p	k	f	a	p
Grass rope	l	g	b	q	l	g	b	q	l	g	b	q	l	g	b	q
Reed	m	h	c	r	m	h	c	r	m	h	c	r	m	h	c	r
Ocelot	n	i	d	s	n	i	d	s	n	i	d	s	n	i	d	s
Eagle	o	j	e	t	o	j	e	t	o	j	e	t	o	j	e	t
Vulture	p	k	f	a	p	k	f	a	p	k	f	a	p	k	f	a
Motion	q	l	g	b	q	l	g	b	q	l	g	b	q	l	g	b
Flint	r	m	h	c	r	m	h	c	r	m	h	c	r	m	h	c
Rain	s	n	i	d	s	n	i	d	s	n	i	d	s	n	i	d
Rose	t	o	j	e	t	o	j	e	t	o	j	e	t	o	j	e

2. The next step is to find the Aztec cycle *number* for your date of birth. This involves a simple calculation. Find the number of your month from this list:

Jan:	1	Apr:	0	July:	0	Oct:	1
Feb:	6	May:	4	Aug:	5	Nov:	6
Mar:	8	June:	9	Sep:	10	Dec:	10

To this, add the day of the month and the last two digits of the year. In our example, 12 February 1957 would give this sum:

$$
\begin{array}{ll}
\text{month number} & = 6 \\
\text{day number} & = 12 \\
\text{year number} & = 57 \\
\hline
\text{Total:} & 75
\end{array}
$$

191

Finally, divide this number by thirteen and the remainder is your Aztec cycle number. In our example, seventy-five divided by thirteen leaves a remainder of ten, so the full Aztec designation for 12 February 1957 is *Ten House*.

The name *House* has already been interpreted as referring to brain and nerve functions. *Ten* may be interpreted from the list below:

Number	*Interpretation*
One	Weakness in the afflicted part, early in life, but passing off later, perhaps in middle age
Two	Pain, but no malfunction of the part
Three	A serious childhood illness connected with this part
Four	Chronic problems in later life from this part, perhaps caused by malfunction or an injury
Five	Generally normal health, or only minor illnesses, connected with this part, especially in youth
Six	Poor health, stemming from some affliction of this part
Seven	Very good health, no weakness in this part
Eight	Poor health in childhood, stemming from some disease of this part, which later clears up
Nine	Generally good health, or only minor illnesses, connected with this part, especially in mature years
Ten	Continuing illness or affliction of this part in childhood and youth, perhaps clearing later
Eleven	A serious illness in later years, connected with this part
Twelve	Pain, especially 'growing pains' of youth, associated with this part, but little or no malfunction
Thirteen	Weakness in the afflicted part, which becomes apparent only late in life

CHAPTER FOUR

Astrology and Biorhythms

In 1969 the Ohmi Railway Company, which runs buses and taxis in two of Japan's most traffic-clogged cities, tried reducing its accident rate by a strange, astrological-sounding experiment. The birth dates of the company's 700 drivers were fed into a computer, which periodically issued warning cards. On a certain day a certain driver would receive a card when he began work, telling him, in effect: 'Today your physical biorhythm is at a critical phase. You are likely to have impaired reaction times. Drive especially carefully.'

The system had been tried already, with success, in the municipal transportation systems of Zürich and Hanover. Ohmi knew this, and also knew that biorhythm patterns were visible in its own accident record. 'Of 331 accidents that had occurred over the five years between 1963 and 1968, 59 per cent had occurred on a driver's critical day, or on the day immediately preceding or following the critical day.'[1]

Ohmi put the system into effect in 1969, and that year its accident rate was halved. It continued to drop in subsequent years, even though the rate for Japan as a whole was going up every year. In 1973, Ohmi clocked up nearly three million miles without a single accident.[2]

The theory of biorhythms began before 1900, in the work of two doctors. In Vienna, Dr Hermann Swoboda began to keep detailed, day-to-day records on certain of his patients' symptoms: inflammation, tissue swelling, pain, fevers, attacks of asthma, the sudden onset of any disease and heart attacks. The accumulation of data allowed him to see hidden cyclic patterns in these symptoms. They occurred most often at intervals of twenty-three days or twenty-eight days, and they could be predicted. Meanwhile in Berlin, Dr Wilhelm

Fliess discovered the same two cycles. Medical scientists had long known of the average menstrual cycle of twenty-eight days in women, but Fliess discovered that men, too, go through a twenty-eight-day cycle, during which they gain and lose weight, undergo hormone changes and find their emotions varying periodically from elation to depression. Fliess also found the basic cycle of twenty-three days operating in both sexes, causing changes in physical energy, alertness, and resistance to disease.

A third biorhythm was discovered at Innsbruck, Austria, by Alfred Teltscher, a doctor of engineering. In studying the performances of students on examinations, he found a 'mental alertness', or intellectual cycle, of thirty-three days.

Figure 22 shows how these three important biorhythms

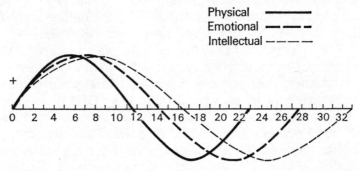

22. Biorhythms at birth, and for the first 33 days of life. The physical rhythm begins a new cycle every 23 days, the emotional cycle every 28 days, and the intellectual cycle every 33 days, throughout the life of the individual.

begin at birth. The short, twenty-three-day physical cycle rises to a peak at the sixth day of life, returns to a critical point at eleven and a half days, hits its lowest point at about seventeen days, and on the twenty-third day is at another critical point, exactly as at the day of birth.

The twenty-eight-day emotional cycle takes five days longer to complete, so that it soon moves 'out of phase' with the twenty-three-day physical cycle, as the longer thirty-three-day intellectual cycle moves out of phase with both of them. In fact, the three are never together at a critical point –

194

as at birth – until over fifty-eight years have elapsed.

The most important days of any cycle are those at the highest peak in the positive half of the cycle, at the lowest trough in the negative half, and at the 'critical' points, when the cycle crosses from positive to negative (or vice versa). It's easy to see why these are important days if we examine each cycle in turn:

The twenty-three-day Physical Cycle. Everyone, every athlete in particular, is aware that there are some days on which his body seems to work better with less effort. These 'peak' days mean quicker reactions, more strength, longer endurance and fitness in general. When Mark Spitz became the first person to win seven Olympic gold medals, during ten days in August and September 1972, his physical cycle was moving through the highest part of its rhythm, and it was perhaps boosted by a high in his emotional cycle. Muhammed Ali was likewise high in both physical and emotional cycles on 25 September 1974, when he defeated George Foreman in Zaire. Foreman was at that time undergoing a physical low.

In general, you should expect to feel as follows in different parts of your physical cycle:

1. High days: energetic, alert, quicker and stronger than at other times, finding a certain enjoyment in physical work, not easily fatigued. But tendency to overwork, if other cycles are 'off'.

2. Low days: tired, listless, not sleeping well, with slow reactions, overwhelmed by physical work, inclined to take it easy.

3. Critical days: during these days your cycle is changing rapidly from positive to negative (or vice versa), making your energy resources and reactions unpredictable. This could mean some danger in driving or operating machinery which requires physical alertness or quick decisions. Misjudgement or sudden fatigue is common.

The twenty-eight-day Emotional Cycle. This is usually characterized by elevated or depressed moods, which can affect physical or mental performance.

195

1. High days: elated, enthusiastic, expressive, extraverted, able to deal with emotional crises at home and at work, good days for almost any activity. But if intellectual and physical cycles are not also high, these could be days of emotional exhaustion.

2. Low days: depressed, quiet, reflective, melancholy, tending to allow emotional problems to get you down, to magnify your troubles. You probably need more sleep than usual at this time, and prefer being alone.

3. Critical days: rapid changeover in your moods could make these days of touchiness and irritability. In particular, you may tend to do things for emotional reasons, and to show poor judgement.

The thirty-three-day Intellectual Cycle. Just as we all have good and bad physical days, or days of elation and depression, we also have days of mental keenness or mental fatigue. Dr Douglas E. Neil of the US Naval Postgraduate School at Monterey, California, tested for this cycle in the exam performances of his students. He predicted above-average scores during the positive phase of each student's intellectual cycle, below-average during the negative phase. This turned out to be the case, in over fourteen months of testing. Three times as many high scores turned up in high days, as in others. Seventy per cent of the low scores occurred during low days.[3]

This cycle has been studied less than the other two, but its profile in your life probably works like this:

1. High days: mental alertness, quickness of thought and coordination, a surge of creativity, problem-solving ability never better. If physical or emotional cycle is critical, however, this could lead to your taking on too much mental work, becoming overtired and suffering from nervous exhaustion.

2. Low days: sluggish thought processes, lack of new ideas, easily stumped by problems you might otherwise tackle cheerfully. These are the days when artists have creative 'blocks', when accountants find their additions going wrong, and when airline pilots make 'stupid' mistakes.

3. Critical days: ups and downs in your mental processes, judgement very unpredictable, thinking may suddenly get stalled. Again, driving or operating machinery that requires quick decisions may be a problem.

Bernard Gittelson's *Biorhythm* lists many more studies of biorhythms, the earliest a report by Hans Schwing in 1939. 'Schwing shows that serious accidents are *five* times more likely to occur when you have a critical day than when you have a day of mixed rhythms.'[4] Days when two, or all three, rhythms are critical are especially dangerous, according to Professor Reinhold Bochow of Humboldt University in Berlin, who studied accidents involving agricultural machinery.[5] Harold R. Willis, a psychologist at Missouri Southern State College studied 200 hospital deaths from 1973. Fifty-six per cent of these deaths took place on a patient's critical day. Among heart-attack victims, sixty-three per cent died on critical days, despite the fact that only twenty per cent of all days are critical.[6]

Other reports indicate recurring fevers and the possibility of spleen disorders, linked to at least two of these same three cycles. Of course thorough research into the links between biorhythms and disease is yet to come, but there certainly seems to be more than a fortuitous link in the medical studies so far.

In general, we ought to expect resistance to disease to be high whenever the rhythms are 'mixed', that is, non-critical. In particular, when physical and emotional rhythms are high, and intellectual rhythm is non-critical, a person's health should be as good as it ever can be – depending of course on his health in general. But days when one, two or all three cycles are critical, seem likely to be days of low resistance to disease.

Figure 23 shows the biorhythm chart of Clark Gable for November 1960. He suffered a heart attack on 5 November, when his physical rhythm was critical. On 16 November, when it was again critical, he suffered a second attack and died. 'His doctor later admitted that the actor's life might

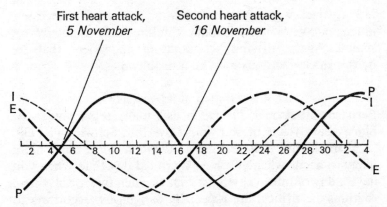

First heart attack, *5 November*

Second heart attack, *16 November*

23. Biorhythms of Clark Gable, November 1960. His first heart attack occurred on the 5th, when his physical cycle (P) was critical. He did not suffer another attack until the 16th, when once more his physical cycle was critical.

have been saved if the needed medical equipment had been in place beside his bed when he was stricken a second time.'[7]

BIORHYTHMS AND SUN SIGNS

In the Sun sign chapters of Part Two above, each sign is associated with certain 'biorhythm risk days', shown as symbols. For example, under Aries, the risk days are:

P	E	I
+	c	c
−	c	c
−	+	c
+	−	c
c	+	−

P stands for the physical cycle, *E* for the emotional cycle, and *I* for the intellectual cycle. High days are marked (+), low days (−) and critical days (c). The five rows of symbols thus represent five types of risk day, when Ariens in particular are likely to experience physical or emotional or mental stress.

The first type of day seems a common-sense suggestion: Ariens should take care on days when, though they may have an abundance of physical energy, their emotions are off-balance and their judgement poor (+, c, c). But this is also a characteristic trouble spot for all persons born under one of the *positive* signs (Aries, Gemini, Leo, Libra, Sagittarius, Aquarius). These signs are traditionally associated with physical energy and 'masculine' traits, just as the six *negative* signs are associated with emotional energy and 'feminine' traits. The negative signs (Taurus, Cancer, Virgo, Scorpio, Capricorn, Pisces) include among their risk days the high-emotion, double-critical day (c, +, c).

The same principle applies to all the signs as grouped by other principles: the four elements, the three natures, the six reflexives and the four seasons. And these groupings explain the five types of risk days for each sign. In Aries, for example,

P	E	I	
+	c	c	for *positive* signs
—	c	c	for Fire signs
—	+	c	for Cardinal signs
+	—	c	for Aries and its reflex, Libra
c	+	—	for Spring signs

The full list for all groupings is:

	P	E	I
1. *The two polarities*:			
Positive	+	c	c
Negative	c	+	c
2. *The four elements*:			
Fire (enthusiastic, hasty)	—	c	c
Earth (methodical, practical)	c	c	—
Air (intellectual, communicative)	c	—	c
Water (emotional, intuitive)	—	+	—
3. *The three natures*:			
Cardinal (enterprising)	—	+	c
Fixed (enduring)	c	—	+
Mutable (changing)	—	c	+
4. *The six reflexives*:			
Aries–Libra	+	—	c
Taurus–Scorpio	+	—	—
Gemini–Sagittarius	c	—	—
Cancer–Capricorn	—	—	+
Leo–Aquarius	—	—	—
Virgo–Pisces	—	—	c

199

5. *The four seasons*:

Spring (Aries, Taurus, Gemini)	c	+	−
Summer (Cancer, Leo, Virgo)	c	c	+
Autumn (Libra, Scorpio, Sagittarius)	−	c	−
Winter (Capricorn, Aquarius, Pisces)	c	c	c

Clark Gable, for example, was born on 1 February 1901, with the Sun in 12° Aquarius. As his biorhythm chart shows (Figure 23), his first heart attack in 1960 occurred when his physical rhythm was critical, his emotional low and his intellectual high. For Aquarians, the risk day (c, −, +) is plainly indicated.

CALCULATING BIORHYTHMS

If you know your Sun sign and wish to check the accuracy of the 'risk day' system, you may wish to calculate your three biorhythms. There are a number of books, devices and services that can help, including:

* The Biostar Electronic Calculator watch, made by Certina of Switzerland. Set by a jeweller, it keeps a continuous running account of all three rhythms.

* The 'Dialgraf', a circular slide rule for biorhythms, invented by George Thommen, who pioneered biorhythm research in the United States.

* Various kits and services from Biorhythm Computers, Inc., 119 West 57 Street, New York 10019.

* *Biorhythm*, by Bernard Gittelson, published by Arco Publishing Co. in the US and by Futura Publications Ltd. in Britain, which includes a simplified charting system for biorhythms.

* Personal computer print-outs of your biorhythms from Biocal Ltd, 27 Church Road, Tunbridge Wells, Kent.

* A 'Biolator' or biorhythm calculator, made by Casio in Britain.

In theory, anyone can calculate his own biorhythms with nothing but pencil and paper. Since each type of cycle repeats itself endlessly, your physical cycle is exactly as it was at your birth on the twenty-third day of life, again on the forty-sixth day, and so on. It's only necessary to know how many complete cycles you've lived through, and how many days on into the next repetition.

But in practice, this means finding out how many days you've lived (exactly), which can be tedious. The easiest do-it-yourself method I know of uses an ordinary pocket calculator.

POCKET CALCULATOR FORMULA FOR BIORHYTHMS

Many people believe they need to consult a sophisticated computer to find out their biorhythm cycles. In fact, you can find out everything about your three important cycles – physical, emotional and intellectual – for any day of your life, using only a pocket calculator (any type will do).

It's easiest to begin with a birthday, and find your twenty-three-day physical cycle:

1. Enter your age at this birthday.
2. Multiply by 365.
3. Using this table, count the number of leap years you have lived through, up to this birthday.

		Leap years			
1904	1920	1936	1952	1968	1984
1908	1924	1940	1956	1972	1988
1912	1928	1944	1960	1976	
1916	1932	1948	1964	1980	

4. Add the number of leap years to your result, and write down the total (or, if your calculator has a memory, store it).
5. Divide by the cycle number (in the physical cycle, 23).
6. The answer will have a whole-number part and a decimal part. Subtract the whole-number part.
7. Multiply by the cycle number (physical, 23) again. The answer gives your position on this cycle, as shown in Figure 24 below. You may care to mark your position on this cycle.
8. Using the total from step (4) above, repeat steps (5), (6) and (7), for the other two biorhythm cycles, but use the appropriate cycle numbers (emotional, 28; intellectual, 33). You now know your exact position on all three cycles, at this birthday.

The calculations for any other day (not a birthday) are almost the same. But in step (4), add also the number of days from the birthday to this day.

Sample Calculation: Someone born 12 February 1957 wishes to find out his biorhythm cycles for 28 March 1979.

1. Age: 22
2. $22 \times 365 = 8030$
3. He has lived through leap years 1960, 1964, 1968, 1972, 1976, or five in all, so:
4. $8030 + 5 = 8035$
   To this, he must add the number of days from his birthday to 28 March, twenty-four days. $8035 + 24 = 8059$
5. For the physical   For the emotional   For the intellectual
   cycle: cycle: cycle:
   $8059/23 = 350 \cdot 39$ $8059/28 = 287 \cdot 82$ $8059/33 = 244 \cdot 21$
6. $350 \cdot 39 - 350 =$ $287 \cdot 82 - 287 =$ $244 \cdot 21 - 244 =$
   $0 \cdot 39$ $0 \cdot 82$ $0 \cdot 21$
7. $0 \cdot 39 \times 23 = 9$ $0 \cdot 82 \times 28 = 23$ $0 \cdot 21 \times 33 = 7$

From Figure 24, it can be seen that his physical rhythm, in the ninth day, is about to become critical; his emotional rhythm, at day twenty-three, is below par, and his intellectual rhythm, at day seven, is high. This would be a good day for light physical activity or hard mental work, but poor for dealing with social or emotional problems, or handling a crisis at work.

OTHER LIFE RHYTHMS: BODY CHARTING

The biorhythm theory would be more convincing if everyone conformed exactly to the three major rhythms one hundred per cent of the time. The fact that sixty-three per cent of heart victims died on critical days in the Missouri study must be balanced with the fact that thirty-seven per cent did not die on critical days. The fact that many athletes perform better on high physical-cycle days does not explain why others turn in record performances on *low* days. Apparently biorhythms apply to some people perfectly, to others approximately, and to others not at all.

This does not mean that the biorhythm theory is wrong.

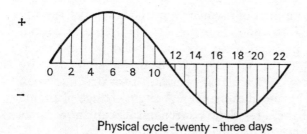

Physical cycle - twenty - three days

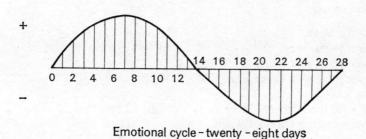

Emotional cycle - twenty - eight days

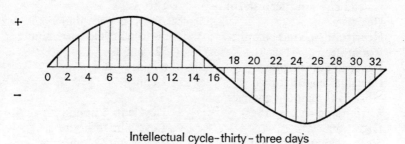

Intellectual cycle - thirty - three days

24. Biorhythm chart. Using this and the formula above, it is possible to see directly which days are high, low or critical (change-over) days.

Rather, it means that statistical averages, worked out for the whole population, cannot apply to every individual. The 'average man' may have a physical cycle of twenty-three days, just as he may have a height of 5 feet, 9·3 inches, but of course this does not mean that every man has the same cycle or the same height.

Human life is regulated by thousands of internal and external rhythms interacting with one another in complex ways. It may be, for example, that the emotional cycle depends upon a number of involved hormone cycles of varying length, as well as upon the action of the Sun and Moon. Likewise the physical cycle may be related to the time it takes the body to rebuild muscle tissue after exercise (about eleven or twelve days), which in turn depends upon a complex of chemical exchanges. A slight change of timing in any one of these regulatory mechanisms can show up as a large difference in the final biorhythm.

A few of the body's internal rhythms are shown in the table below.

Body Rhythm	Timing
Cerebral neurones	1000 cycles per second
Slower brain neurones, associated with perception	50 cps
Brain waves:	
beta rhythm (frontal lobe)	18 to 22 cps
alpha rhythm (present when eyes are closed)	8 to 13 cps
theta rhythm (memory, half-sleep)	4 to 7 cps
delta rhythm (deep sleep)	1 to 3 cps
Heartbeat	76 cycles per minute
Heartbeat (second chamber)	50 to 60 cycles per minute
Respiration	22 cpm
Stomach contractions	3 cpm
Intestinal contractions	1 cpm
Nostrils (breathing changes from one to the other)	1 cycle in 6 hours
Digestion	1 cycle in 18 hours
Sleep, temperature, kidneys	1 cycle in 24 hours
Muscle tissue replacement	11 to 12 days
Ovulation	28 days
Red blood cell replacement	128 days
Bone calcium replacement	200 days
Gestation	266 days

Most people find that from day to day they undergo significant changes not only in mood, physical stamina and intellectual acuity, but in a variety of body activities: One night you may need an extra hour's sleep, while another brings insomnia. Your appetite may vary from virtual gluttony to almost no desire for food. Your weight may go up or down a pound from day to day. Factors like moodiness, alertness, euphoria or depression may even vary from hour to hour.

Often such variations are cyclical, but this can only be discovered by charting them on a day-to-day basis. Body charting is the system recommended by various writers on biorhythms.[8] It consists simply of preparing a list of questions, about your body activities, then answering these questions daily and recording your answers in a diary. Most patterns will emerge within three to six months, although some may become apparent within a week.

The following list of questions is meant to suggest a suitable list for your personal body chart. To make the chart effective, only the first question in each category need be answered daily. Adding other questions will of course improve your chances of finding body rhythms too subtle to be caught by the main questions.

Body Rhythm Chart (to be marked daily)
A. Sleeping
   1. How many hours did I sleep last night?
   2. What time did I settle down for sleep?
   3. How long did it take me to fall asleep?
   4. Did I sleep well, or poorly?
   5. Did I have trouble waking up?
   6. Did I take a nap today?
     (a) When?
     (b) For how long?
   7. How did I feel most of the day:
     (a) Very tired
     (b) Tired
     (c) Normal
     (d) Alert
     (e) Energetic
B. Eating
   1. At what times did I feel hungry today?
   2. At what times did I eat?
   3. Would I describe my appetite as:
     (a) Ravenous

205

(b) Quite good
(c) Normal
(d) Poor
(e) No appetite
4. At what time did I eat my largest meal?
5. What type of food did I eat mainly, or most often?
(a) Meat and fish
(b) Milk, eggs, dairy products (unsweetened)
(c) Cereal, bread, potatoes, legumes
(d) Other vegetables
(e) Fruit
(f) Sweets and sweet foods
6. Vitamins or food supplements taken
7. Estimate of today's calories

C. Activity
1. Would I describe this day as physically or sexually:
(a) very active
(b) normal
(c) less active than usual
(d) almost no activity
2. Any sexual activity? At what time of day?
3. Physical activity:
(a) none, or almost none
(b) normal work routine or usual exercise
(c) light exercise in addition to usual routine (e.g calis-
    thenics, golf, bowling, swimming)
(d) hard exercise (eg, running, weightlifting)
4. At the end of the day, did I feel physically exhausted?

D. Health
1. Was I well today?
2. How much did I weigh this morning?
3. Bowel movement:
(a) Constipated
(b) Normal
(c) Diarrhoea
4. Aches or pains:
(a) Continuing
(b) New
(c) Ceasing

5. Location of pain:
    (a) head
    (b) back
    (c) abdomen
    (d) elsewhere
6. Any illness or symptom characteristic of my Sun sign (see pp. 79–142)?
7. Any other illness or symptom today?

E. Mood
1. How would I describe my mood for most of the day?
    (a) Energetic or weary?
    (b) Happy or depressed?
    (c) Relaxed or nervous?
    (d) Aggressive or passive?
    (e) Bored or enthusiastic?
    (f) Sparkling or mentally stale?
    (g) Irritated or calm?
    (h) Self-centred or outgoing?
    (i) Serious or frivolous?
    (j) Self-confident or shy?
    (k) Creative or destructive?
    (l) Absent-minded or alert?
2. Any sudden change of mood during the day?
3. Did I handle any crisis well?
4. How did I feel the day went?
    (a) Began badly and ended well
    (b) Began well and ended badly
    (c) Couldn't have been better
    (d) Couldn't have been worse
    (e) Fairly ordinary day
5. Did I daydream or fantasize today?
    (a) enjoyable fantasy
    (b) worrisome or unenjoyable fantasy
6. Any trouble at home or with loved ones?
7. Any trouble at work?
8. Was this a day I'd like to remember? Why (or why not)?
9. Did I feel well in control of my moods today?

APPENDIX A

*Homeopathic Remedies**

Note: This list is for information only. Many of the substances listed are poisonous, and of course all drugs are dangerous unless taken under medical supervision.

Aries:	aconite, calcium lactate, camphor
Taurus:	brionia alba, calcium carbonate, belladonna
Gemini:	sodium phosphate, carb. veg., potassium iodide
Cancer:	arnica, salol, rhus toxica, bismuth carbonate
Leo:	china, sodium sulphate, convally, nux vom.
Virgo:	calcium carbonate, caffeine, carb. veg.
Libra:	sodium bicarbonate, arsenicum album, ferr. red
Scorpio:	gelsemine, sec. corn, sulphur
Sagittarius:	sepia, phenolphthalein, carb. veg., copper
Capricorn:	ign. ammonium, colchicum, graphite
Aquarius:	arsenicum album, brionia alba, potassium iodide, silac
Pisces:	vertrum, ferr. lactate, magnesium sulphate

* Derived from those given in Maurice Ernest, *Everyday Chronic Maladies* (London: Adam & Co., n.d.) and in Omar V. Garrison, *Medical Astrology* (New York: Warner Paperback Library, 1973).

APPENDIX B

*Traditional Herbs**

Many medicinal 'discoveries' of our time were in use long before Western doctors knew of them. The Indians of Peru had been preparing a tea from the bark of the cinchona tree for many centuries, and giving it to yellow fever victims. Jesuit missionaries brought it to us as *quinine*. The same infusion had another ingredient, *quinidine*, not officially discovered until 1914, when East Indians used it to calm the heart murmur of a Dutch sea captain. Today it is a standard drug.

Two thousand years ago the Brahmin priests achieved a calm state of mind by taking *Rauwolfia serpentina*, a plant root which lowers blood pressure – today it does the same for millions of sufferers from high blood pressure all over the world. *Digitalis*, prepared from the dried leaves of the *Digitalis purpurea* plant, was a cure for dropsy in England for centuries; dropsy is heart failure, and digitalis increases the efficiency of the heart muscles (just how it does this is still unknown).

A visit to the pharmacist will yield dozens of other ancient remedies, still in use in 'respectable' medicine: Throat pastilles? An Egyptian derivative from the jujube tree. Tonics? Known to the Pythagoreans. Even the humble aspirin (salicylic acid) was known to the ancient Celts of Britain, as the active principle in willow sap. The Ebers Papyrus of Egypt (*c.* 1500 BC) lists over 700 remedies, many of them familiar today (eg, castor oil).

How were all these and many thousands of other folk

* Ancient herbs included in modern pharmacopoeia are mentioned in some detail in Richard Burack, *The Handbook of Prescription Drugs* (New York: Pantheon, 1967).

remedies first discovered? Certainly not by any random 'trial and error' method: Since many of these drugs are poisonous, random trials would be more dangerous than the diseases they cure. Brian Inglis writes of a possible method: 'There is an old tag in Celtic lore to the effect that a curative herb ought not to be looked for if it is to be found; instinct will guide the sick man to the appropriate plant.'*

This sounds like a reasonable method. A dog or cat can often cure itself of some common ailment by chewing what it needs. Animals in the wild are also sensitive to what's good for them. Humans cannot have lost this instinct entirely, and the proof is in the great number of herbal remedies found, all over the world.

'Instinct' here may well mean astral influence. Since plants and humans both interact with cosmic forces, they may be interacting with each other. This hypothetical communication system between man and plant† could work like this: Suppose that an ailing person puts out a low-energy signal characteristic of his disease. Suppose also that a particular plant of curative value puts out a complementary signal. Locating the herb would then become a matter of 'tuning in on the right frequency', a kind of instinctive, sixth-sense behaviour observed in dowsers. The herb leads the ailing person to it.

Such a hypothesis is difficult to test, but not altogether unlikely. The fact is that plants respond to the movements of the solar system, and so does human health – it should be no surprise if the two are keyed together.

This three-way interaction between plants, planets and patients may explain why lists of herbs under astrological signs are different if these lists are prepared in different parts of the world. Obviously a common plant like sage does not bloom at the same time in Greece as in Britain, so its potency will appear under a different sign. As the following list shows, there are some real discrepancies between herbals from different places.

* Brian Inglis, *Fringe Medicine* (London: Faber, 1964), p. 72.
† This system is discussed fully in P. Tomkins & C. Bird, *The Secret Life of Plants* (Harmondsworth: Penguin, 1975).

Sign	Greek herb*	Remarks
Aries	sage	(British sage is Taurean)
	water milfoil	
Taurus	vervain	(British vervain and clover are
	clover	Geminian)
Gemini	holy vervain	
	gladiolus	
Cancer	comfrey	(British comfrey is Capricornian)
	mandrake	
Leo	cyclamen	
Virgo	calamint	(in Britain, assigned to Virgo's
		planet, Mercury)
Libra	scorpion-tail	
Sagittarius	pimpernel	
Capricorn	sorrel	(British sorrel is Taurean)
Aquarius	fennel	(British fennel is Virgoan)
	buttercup	
Pisces	birthwort	

* Greek herbs from Rupert Gleadow, *Origin of the Zodiac* (London: Cape, 1968), p. 85.

Notes

PART ONE

Chapter One. Zodiac Man

1. See J. A. West and J. Toonder, *The Case for Astrology* (London: Macdonald, 1970), plates 12a, 12b, pp. 144–5
2. James Vogh, *Arachne Rising*, pp. 13–15; J. F. Goodavage, *Write Your Own Horoscope* (New York: New American Library, 1968), pp. 27–8; *News of the World*, 24 August 1975
3. West and Toonder, *The Case for Astrology*, p. 170, citing F. A. Brown, article in *Nature*, 4 December 1959
4. Lyall Watson, *Supernature* (London: Coronet, 1973), p. 25
5. Ibid., pp. 10–11, 43ff
6. Ibid., p. 46
7. John Ivimy, *The Sphinx and the Megaliths* (London: Abacus, 1976), p. 77, quoting Geoffrey of Monmouth. See also *Geoffrey of Monmouth's History of the Kings of Britain*, Sebastian Evans trans. (London: Dent, 1904)
8. Joseph F. Goodavage, *Write Your Own Horoscope*, p. 245, quoting Hippocrates
9. Claudius Ptolemy, *Tetrabiblos*, F. E. Robbins trans. (London: William Heinemann, 1971), pp. 193, 211ff, 321
10. Edward R. Dewey, *Cycles* (New York: Hawthorn Books, 1971), p. 151
11. Goodavage, op. cit., p. 85
12. Geoffrey of Monmouth, op. cit., quoted in *A Pictorial and Descriptive Guide to Bath*, 10th edn. (London: Ward Lock & Co., n.d.), p. 27
13. Ibid., p. 69
14. John Michell, *The View over Atlantis* (London: Abacus, 1975), p. 15; Alfred Watkins, *The Old Straight Track* (London: Abacus, 1974), preface to 1925 edn.
15. Colin Wilson, *Strange Powers* (London: Abacus, 1975), pp. 18–19

16. Zoë Tasré, *Earth's Children* (Bristol: Aegon Press, n.d.), p. 113
17. Adi-Kent Thomas Jeffrey, *The Bermuda Triangle* (London: W. H. Allen, 1975), pp. 131–4
18. Frank Edwards, *Stranger than Science* (London: Pan, 1963), p. 118
19. P. F. Browne, 'The Llandudno Pentagon', in *New Scientist*, 1 April 1977, vol. 73, no. 1045, pp. 784–5
20. Guy Underwood, *The Pattern of the Past* (London: Abacus, 1972)
21. Colin Wilson, 'Star Lores', in *Sunday Times Magazine*, 2 October 1977, pp. 25–30
22. See Note 1 above

Chapter Two. The Sun

1. After K. Sethe, *Amun und die acht Urgötter*, quoted in Henri Frankfort, *Ancient Egyptian Religion* (New York: Harper & Row, 1948), p. 27.
2. E. N. Parker, 'The Sun', in *Scientific American*, September 1975, p. 43
3. Lyall Watson, *Supernature*, p. 53
4. J. Poumailloux and R. Viart, 'Corrélations possibles entre l'incidence des infarctus du myocarde et l'augmentation des activités solaires et géomagnétiques', in *Bulletin d'Académie de la Médecine*, 1959, vol. 143, p. 167
5. E. M. Dewey, *Cycles*, p. 74
6. John Michell, op. cit., p. 140; John Ivimy, op. cit., pp. 116–40
7. Lyall Watson, op. cit., p. 100
8. Ibid.
9. J. A. West and J. Toonder, *The Case for Astrology*, p. 33
10. J. Mayo, O. White and H. J. Eysenck, 'An Empirical Study of the Relation between Astrological Factors and Personality' (to be published)

Chapter Three. The Moon

1. Lyall Watson, op. cit., p. 30
2. D. Bradley, M. Woodbury and G. Brier, 'Lunar Synodical Period and Widespread Precipitation', in *Science*, 1962, no. 137, p. 748
3. Watson, op. cit., p. 50
4. Derek and Julia Parker, *The Compleat Astrologer* (London: Mitchell Beazley, 1975), p. 57

5. S. Ostrander and L. Schroeder, *PSI: Psychic Discoveries behind the Iron Curtain* (London: Abacus, 1973), pp. 350–53
6. A. Rosenblum and L. Jackson, *The Natural Birth Control Book* (Boston: Tao Publications, 1974), pp. 15–18
7. Ibid., p. 11
8. Ostrander and Schroeder, op. cit., p. 353
9. Rosenblum and Jackson, op. cit., pp. 92–5
10. Ostrander and Schroeder, op. cit., p. 353
11. W. and A. Menaker, 'Lunar Periodicity in Human Reproduction', in *American Journal of Obstetrical Gynaecology*, 1959, vol. 78, p. 905
12. J. F. Goodavage, op. cit., p. 33
13. Ibid.
14. Colin Wilson, 'Night of the Full Moon', in *Men Only*, vol. 39, no. 12, p. 11
15. Ibid.
16. Lyall Watson, *Supernature*, p. 57
17. Robert Graves, *The White Goddess* (London: Faber, 1961), p. 490

Chapter Four. Planet Rhythms

1. J. Revill, 'The Two Tone Horoscope of Shirley MacLaine, Fascinator', in *Prediction*, January 1976, p. 7
2. A. Singer and E. A. Underwood, *A Short History of Medicine*, 2nd edn. (Oxford: Clarendon Press, 1962), p. 187
3. Colin Wilson, *The Occult* (London: Mayflower, 1973), p. 32
4. Singer and Underwood, loc. cit.
5. West and Toonder, op. cit., p. 167

Chapter Five. The Wheel of Life

1. Michel Gauquelin, *Cosmic Influences on Human Behaviour* (London: Garnstone Press, 1973), pp. 40–60
2. Ibid., p. 144

PART TWO
Reading the Medical Horoscope

1. D. Parker and J. Parker, *The Compleat Astrologer* (London: Mitchell Beazley, 1975); C. E. O. Carter, *The Principles of Astrology* (London and Bombay: Theosophical Publishing House, n.d.); C. Ptolemy, *Tetrabiblos*, translated from the Greek by F. E. Robbins, (London: William Heinemann,

1940); many other guides are available

2. Joseph F. Goodavage, *Write Your Own Horoscope* (New York: N.A.L., 1968); Max Heindel, *Simplified Scientific Astrology* (Oceanside, Calif.: Rosicrucian Fellowship, 1938)

Chapter Thirteen. Arachne

1. James Vogh, *Arachne Rising* (London: Hart–Davis, Mac-Gibbon, 1977)

2. Russell Targ and Harold Puthoff, 'Information Transmission under Sensory Shielding', in *Nature*, vol. 251, 18 October 1974, pp. 602–7

3. N. L. Browning, *The Psychic World of Peter Hurkos* (London: Frederick Muller, 1972), pp. 73–88

4. For a complete description, see A. Hardy, R. Harvie and A. Koestler, *The Challenge of Chance* (London: Hutchinson, 1973)

5. S. Ostrander and L. Schroeder, *PSI: Psychic Discoveries behind the Iron Curtain* (London: Abacus, 1973), pp. 31–44

6. For a complete account of these fascinating experiments, see M. Ullman, S. Krippner and A. Vaughan, *Dream Telepathy* (London: Turnstone Books, 1973)

7. James Vogh, *Arachne Rising*, pp. 109–13

8. Ibid.

9. N. L. Browning, op. cit., pp. 64–71

10. Colin Wilson, *Strange Powers* (London: Abacus, 1975), pp. 27–64

11. Colin Wilson, *The Occult* (London: Mayflower, 1973), p. 131

12. Quoted in Denis Bardens, *Mysterious Worlds* (London: Fontana, 1972), p. 103

13. Quoted in Hardy, Harvie & Koestler, *The Challenge of Chance*

14. Denis Bardens, op. cit., p. 69

15. Ibid., p. 36

16. Ibid., p. 110

PART THREE

Chapter Two. The Aspects

1. Howard Cornell, *Encyclopedia of Medical Astrology* (Los Angeles: 1936); Dal Lee, *Dictionary of Astrology* (New York: Warner Paperback Library, 1968); Omar V. Garrison, *Medical Astrology* (New York: Warner Paperback Library, 1973); C. Norman Shealy, *Occult Medicine Can Save Your*

Life (New York: Dial Press, 1975); Ptolemy, *Tetrabiblos*; Michel Gauquelin, *The Cosmic Clocks* (New York: Avon, 1969); Giorgio Piccardi, *The Chemical Basis of Medical Climatology* (Springfield, Illinois: Charles Thomas, 1962); D. and J. Parker, *The Compleat Astrologer*

2. Dr J. Gomez, *A Dictionary of Symptoms* (London: Paladin, 1970), p. 414
3. S. Ostrander and L. Schroeder, *PSI: Psychic Discoveries behind the Iron Curtain* (London: Abacus, 1970), p. 353
4. Ibid.
5. Ibid., pp. 350–57; see also A. Rosenblum & L. Jackson, *The Natural Birth Control Book* (Boston: Tao Publications, 1974)

PART FOUR

Chapter One. Vedic Astrology and Health

1. For a complete discussion, see Rupert Gleadow, *The Origin of the Zodiac* (London: Cape, 1968) and *Your Character in the Zodiac* (London: Phoenix House, 1968)
2. M. K. Gandhi, 'Indian Medical Astrology' in Garrison, *Medical Astrology*, p. 249
3. Gleadow, *The Origin of the Zodiac*, p. 29
4. Ptolemy, *Tetrabiblos*, iii, 12, p. 325
5. Chandrasekhar, G. Thakkur, *An Introduction to Medical Astrology* (Bombay: Ancient Wisdom, n.d.), pp. 28–9
6. Ibid.
7. Gleadow, *The Origin of the Zodiac*, pp. 137–51
8. Chandrasekhar, *Introduction*, pp. 40–5

Chapter Two. Chinese Astrology and the Life Force

1. Stephan Pálos, *The Chinese Art of Healing* (New York: Bantam, 1972), p. 11
2. Gleadow, *The Origin of the Zodiac*, pp. 95–9
3. Ibid.
4. Pálos, *The Chinese Art of Healing*, p. 10
5. Ibid., p. 8
6. George Gamow, *A Star Called the Sun* (New York: Bantam, 1965), p. 162
7. C. Norman Shealy, *Occult Medicine Can Save Your Life* (New York: Dial, 1975), p. 117
8. Brian Inglis, *Fringe Medicine* (London: Faber, 1964), p. 125

9. Nicholas Culpeper, *The Complete Herbal* (London: Foulsham, 1917); Chinese herbs from list in Pálos, *The Chinese Art of Healing*, pp. 185–9

Chapter Three. Aztec Astrology and Life Cycles

1. F. Nuñez de la Vega, pastoral letter, quoted in Gleadow, *The Origin of the Zodiac*, p. 111
2. These illustrations are reproduced in G. C. Vaillant, *Aztecs of Mexico* (Harmondsworth: Penguin, 1950), pp. 208–9, plates 34–5
3. See Bernard Ortiz de Montellano, 'Empirical Aztec Medicine', in *Science*, vol. 188, no. 4185, 18 April 1975, pp. 214–20
4. Vaillant, *Aztecs of Mexico*, pp. 160–1, plate 12, shows this temple. It is further discussed in my *Arachne Rising*, pp. 29–30
5. *Arachne Rising*, Chapters 1–7, goes into this thirteen-part division of the year more thoroughly
6. According to Immanuel Velikovsky, *Worlds in Collision* (New York: Dell, 1967), pp. 258–9
7. Vaillant, *Aztecs of Mexico*, p. 187
8. Calendar information is from Ibid., pp. 194–204; medical information and figure from Garret Mallery, *Picture-Writing of the American Indians*, vol. 2 (New York: Dover, 1972), pp. 613–14
9. Vaillant, op. cit., pp. 194–204
10. Mallery, op. cit., p. 613

Chapter Four. Astrology and Biorhythms

1. Bernard Gittelson, *Biorhythm* (London: Futura, 1976), p. 53
2. Ibid., p. 54
3. Ibid., pp. 50–2
4. Ibid., p. 3
5. Ibid., p. 32
6. Ibid., pp. 34–5
7. Ibid., p. 1
8. Notably, Gay Luce, *Body Time* (New York: Pantheon, 1971); M. Karlins and L. M. Andrews, *Biofeedback* (London: Abacus, 1975)

List of Illustrations

Index

222

Vaccination, 60
Vedic astrology, 169–75
Venus, 51–2; and Aztec
    calendar, 187; diseases,
    149–50
Virgo, 14, 23–5, 32–6, 52,
    104–108

Water signs, 34
Watson, L., 18, 30

Westmoreland, 13
Wilson, C., 22, 58, 139

Yeats, W. B., 139–40
Yin-yang, 35

Zodiac, 13–16, 23, 41; structure,
    32–6; zodiac man, 13–14,
    53; sidereal, 169–71;
    tropical, 169–71 (*see also*
    names of individual signs)